GOVERNMENT PROCEDURES AND OPERATIONS

FREE EXERCISE OF RELIGION BY CLOSELY HELD CORPORATIONS

THE SUPREME COURT DECISION ON HOBBY LOBBY STORES AND ITS IMPLICATIONS

GOVERNMENT PROCEDURES AND OPERATIONS

Additional books in this series can be found on Nova's website under the Series tab.

Additional e-books in this series can be found on Nova's website under the e-book tab.

GOVERNMENT PROCEDURES AND OPERATIONS

FREE EXERCISE OF RELIGION BY CLOSELY HELD CORPORATIONS

THE SUPREME COURT DECISION ON HOBBY LOBBY STORES AND ITS IMPLICATIONS

AUBREY BOONE
EDITOR

New York

Library of Congress Cataloging-in-Publication Data

ISBN: 978-1-61122-062-9

Published by Nova Science Publishers, Inc. † New York

CONTENTS

PREFACE

One of the ongoing controversies related to the Affordable Care Act (ACA) has been the scope of exemption from certain health care coverage requirements, including the contraceptive coverage requirement. Though closely divided, the U.S. Supreme Court's 5-4 decision in *Burwell v. Hobby Lobby Stores, Inc.* has settled the question of whether certain for-profit corporations must be exempt from the requirement, unless Congress chooses to amend the statute providing those corporations legal protection. This book analyzes the Court's opinions in Hobby Lobby, examining the rights of closely held corporations under the Religious Freedom Restoration Act. It also addresses the implications for the contraceptive coverage mandate under ACA and discusses potential legislative responses to the Court's decision. Finally, it analyzes the impact that Hobby Lobby may have in other contexts in which employers may claim religious objections.

Chapter 1 – A 5-4 decision, issued over a highly critical dissent, *Burwell v. Hobby Lobby Stores, Inc.* resolved one of the many challenges raised in response to the contraceptive coverage requirement of the Affordable Care Act (ACA). Imputing the beliefs of owners of closely held corporations to such corporations, the U.S. Supreme Court found that closely held corporations that hold religious objections to certain contraceptive services cannot be required to provide coverage of those services in employee health plans. The Court's decision was based on the protections offered under the federal Religious Freedom Restoration Act (RFRA), a statute prohibiting the government from imposing a substantial burden on a person's religious exercise unless it can show a compelling interest achieved by the least restrictive means. The Court declined to address the constitutional challenge, holding that the companies were protected under RFRA.

In the absence of a definition under RFRA, the majority interpreted the term "person" to include closely held corporations, even if they operated for-profit, and determined that the penalties that such companies would face if they failed to comply with the contraceptive coverage requirement would impose a substantial burden. Though the Court assumed that the government had a compelling interest to require contraceptive coverage under ACA, it found that less restrictive means (e.g., expanding the regulatory accommodation available to nonprofit employers with similar objections) could achieve that interest without requiring companies with religious objections to be subject to the requirement.

Although *Hobby Lobby* resolved the question regarding the applicability of RFRA to closely held corporations—defined by the Court as "each owned and controlled by members of a single family"—the decision leaves open a number of questions about the scope of RFRA's protections and future enforcement of the contraceptive coverage requirement. Because the Court's decision was based on statutory grounds, Congress remains free to define which entities may be governed by ACA or other federal laws generally.

This report analyzes the Court's decision in *Hobby Lobby*, including arguments made between the majority and dissent, to clarify the scope of the decision and potential impacts for future interpretation of RFRA's applicability. It also examines potential legislative responses, should Congress consider addressing the current applicability of RFRA. Finally, the report addresses the decision's effect on requirements that employers offer contraceptive coverage in group health plans under federal or state law.

Chapter 2 – This is Decision of the Supreme Court of the United States in the case of Burwell, Secretary of Health and Human Services et al., v. Hobby Lobby Stores, Inc., date on June 30, 2014.

In: Free Exercise
Editor: Aubrey Boone

ISBN: 978-1-61122-062-9

Chapter 1

FREE EXERCISE OF RELIGION BY CLOSELY HELD CORPORATIONS: IMPLICATIONS OF *BURWELL V. HOBBY LOBBY STORES, INC.**

Cynthia Brougher

SUMMARY

A 5-4 decision, issued over a highly critical dissent, *Burwell v. Hobby Lobby Stores, Inc.* resolved one of the many challenges raised in response to the contraceptive coverage requirement of the Affordable Care Act (ACA). Imputing the beliefs of owners of closely held corporations to such corporations, the U.S. Supreme Court found that closely held corporations that hold religious objections to certain contraceptive services cannot be required to provide coverage of those services in employee health plans. The Court's decision was based on the protections offered under the federal Religious Freedom Restoration Act (RFRA), a statute prohibiting the government from imposing a substantial burden on a person's religious exercise unless it can show a compelling interest achieved by the least restrictive means. The Court declined to address the constitutional challenge, holding that the companies were protected under RFRA.

In the absence of a definition under RFRA, the majority interpreted the term "person" to include closely held corporations, even if they

---

* This is an edited, reformatted and augmented version of a Congressional Research Service publication, No. R43654, dated July 23, 2014.

operated for-profit, and determined that the penalties that such companies would face if they failed to comply with the contraceptive coverage requirement would impose a substantial burden. Though the Court assumed that the government had a compelling interest to require contraceptive coverage under ACA, it found that less restrictive means (e.g., expanding the regulatory accommodation available to nonprofit employers with similar objections) could achieve that interest without requiring companies with religious objections to be subject to the requirement.

Although *Hobby Lobby* resolved the question regarding the applicability of RFRA to closely held corporations—defined by the Court as "each owned and controlled by members of a single family"—the decision leaves open a number of questions about the scope of RFRA's protections and future enforcement of the contraceptive coverage requirement. Because the Court's decision was based on statutory grounds, Congress remains free to define which entities may be governed by ACA or other federal laws generally.

This report analyzes the Court's decision in *Hobby Lobby*, including arguments made between the majority and dissent, to clarify the scope of the decision and potential impacts for future interpretation of RFRA's applicability. It also examines potential legislative responses, should Congress consider addressing the current applicability of RFRA. Finally, the report addresses the decision's effect on requirements that employers offer contraceptive coverage in group health plans under federal or state law.

One of the ongoing controversies related to the Affordable Care Act (ACA) has been the scope of exemption from certain health care coverage requirements, including the contraceptive coverage requirement.[1] Though closely divided, the U.S. Supreme Court's 5-4 decision in *Burwell v. Hobby Lobby Stores, Inc.* has settled the question of whether certain for-profit corporations must be exempt from the requirement, unless Congress chooses to amend the statute providing those corporations legal protection.[2] Imputing the beliefs of owners of closely held corporations to the corporations themselves, the Court found that the ACA could not require such companies to provide contraceptive coverage in group health plans offered to their employees. It based its decision on the Religious Freedom Restoration Act (RFRA) which provides heightened protection for burdens on religious exercise.[3] Although the case has been analogized to *Citizens United v. Federal Election Commission*, a 2010 case holding that corporations have free speech rights under the First Amendment, the *Hobby Lobby* decision was not decided on constitutional grounds.[4] Instead, it provides protection on a statutory basis, meaning that Congress has the ability to respond to the decision if it disagrees with the Court's ruling.

This report analyzes the Court's opinions in *Hobby Lobby*, examining the rights of closely held corporations under the Religious Freedom Restoration Act. It also addresses the implications for the contraceptive coverage mandate under ACA and discusses potential legislative responses to the Court's decision. Finally, it analyzes the impact that *Hobby Lobby* may have in other contexts in which employers may claim religious objections.

RIGHTS OF CLOSELY HELD CORPORATIONS UNDER THE RELIGIOUS FREEDOM RESTORATION ACT

The companies challenging the contraceptive coverage requirement alleged violation of their religious exercise rights under both the First Amendment's Free Exercise Clause and RFRA. The Free Exercise Clause prohibits the government from prohibiting the free exercise of religion.[5] Traditionally it had been interpreted to require that the government show a compelling interest for any government action that interfered with a person's exercise of religious beliefs.[6] However, in 1990, the Supreme Court reinterpreted that standard, explaining that the Free Exercise Clause never "relieve[s] an individual of the obligation to comply with a valid and neutral law of general applicability."[7]

The Court's decision lowered the baseline of protection, but emphasized that Congress remained free to consider whether additional protection would be appropriate through the legislative process.[8] Congress responded to the Court's decision by enacting RFRA, which essentially reinstated the heightened standard of protection.

RFRA states that the "[g]overnment shall not substantially burden a person's exercise of religion even if the burden results from a rule of general applicability, except as provided in subsection (b)."[9] Subsection (b) requires that any substantial burden must further a compelling governmental interest and use the least restrictive means to achieve that interest.[10]

Threshold Issues: Defining Person and Exercise of Religion

RFRA's language indicates that in order to raise a claim under the statute, "a person's exercise of religion" must be affected. However, when enacting RFRA, Congress never defined the term *person* for purposes of the act. Only if a court determines that the party challenging the government's action is "a person" under the terms of the statute and that the party exercises religion, can the court address the merits of the case—whether an improper substantial burden has been placed on that party.

One of the most significant points of the *Hobby Lobby* decision was its declaration that closely held corporations are "persons" eligible for protection under RFRA. The Court noted the absence of a statutory definition of *person* under RFRA and consequently relied upon the Dictionary Act to ascertain the default meaning of the term.[11] The Dictionary Act defines *person* to "include corporations, companies, associations, firms, partnerships, societies, and joint stock companies, as well as individuals."[12]

Rejecting the assertion that businesses organized as corporations are divested of RFRA's protections, the majority wrote that "[t]he plain terms of RFRA make it perfectly clear that Congress did not discriminate [with regard to the business structure chosen by owners] who wish to run their businesses as for-profit corporation in the manner required by their religious beliefs."[13] The Court reasoned that RFRA was enacted to provide broad protection for religious liberty and, without a specifically applicable definition provided in RFRA, explained that the definition of person was not limited by for-profit status:

> No known understanding of the term 'person' includes some but not all corporations. The term "person" sometimes encompasses artificial persons..., and it sometimes is limited to natural persons. But no conceivable definition of the term includes natural persons and nonprofit corporations, but not for-profit corporations.[14]

The majority acknowledged that the threshold issue arguably is conditioned on the person's ability to exercise religion, a point emphasized by the dissent.[15] However, the majority cited previous cases in which the Court had recognized claims involving exercise of religion of individuals who owned for-profit businesses as sole proprietorships[16] and nonprofit corporations.[17] Despite the dissent's argument that religious corporations could be distinguished from for-profit corporations because they "foster the interests of persons subscribing to the same religious faith," the majority held that the Court's precedent indicated that neither for-profit status nor corporate status are prohibitive factors in analysis of an organization's rights under RFRA.[18]

Notably, when responding to concerns that applying RFRA to for-profit corporations would raise challenges of ascertaining "the religious identity of large, publicly traded corporations," the majority emphasized that its decision applied only to such companies as the ones challenging the contraceptive coverage requirement in this case. In effect, the decision therefore is limited to "closely held corporations, each owned and controlled by members of a single family."[19] Additionally, the majority alluded to the general requirement inherent to religious exercise cases that the parties must base their challenge on sincerely held religious beliefs, meaning that even if RFRA would apply to a particular entity, if the entity is asserting a religious belief for the convenience of avoiding compliance with an unpopular mandate, it could not claim legal protection.[20] The sincerity of the companies' beliefs in *Hobby Lobby* was not disputed.

Although the majority noted that it was recognizing RFRA's applicability to closely held corporations only, it did not foreclose the possibility that in a future case, a court may extend RFRA protection to other types of corporations such as those which are publicly traded. Instead it suggested only that "it seems unlikely" that such "corporate giants" would assert RFRA rights and that "numerous practical restraints would likely prevent that from occurring."[21] The dissent was highly critical of this point, characterizing the decision as one of "startling breadth:"[22]

> The Court's determination that RFRA extends to for-profit corporations is bound to have untoward effects. Although the Court attempts to cabin its language to closely held corporations, its logic extends to corporations of any size, public or private.[23]

Indeed the dissent's argument that the decision may provide a basis for expanding the protection of RFRA further in the future may reasonably give pause. As noted, the majority did not preclude future application of RFRA to a broader range of corporations, using tentative language and noting a lack of obvious challenges. Furthermore, the majority's explanation that the Dictionary Act's definition of person could not be read to distinguish between types of corporations related to the company's profit status suggests that it also may not be read to distinguish between types of corporations on other grounds (e.g., size or public trading status).

Prohibition on Substantial Burden

After determining that RFRA's protections would apply, the Court examined the merits of the RFRA claim, first identifying the burden that compliance with the contraceptive coverage mandate would impose on the companies challenging the mandate. According to the Court, requiring the owners of the companies to arrange for "health insurance that covers methods of birth control that ... may result in the destruction of an embryo" means that the "mandate demands that they engage in conduct that seriously violates their religious beliefs."[24]

If the owners were to refuse to comply with the demand, the companies would face penalties under the ACA that the Court characterized as "surely substantial."[25] If the companies continued to provide their preferred health coverage without including the mandated contraceptive coverage, they would face penalties each day of noncompliance, ranging from $40,000 per day to $1.3 million per day.[26] If the companies stopped providing any insurance coverage to avoid covering contraceptives and avoid the consequent daily penalties, they would risk paying a different penalty under ACA, which could range from $800,000 per year to $26 million per year.[27]

The majority recognized the substantial burden arising from the owners' religious objections and potential financial penalties over strong objection from the dissenting Justices. Justice Ginsburg, who authored the principal dissent, criticized the majority's assessment as equating a sincere religious objection with a substantial burden, instead of distinguishing between the two.[28] In other words, simply because a government mandate conflicts with a person's religious belief, the mandate is not necessarily a substantial burden. The dissent explained that the relationship between the belief and the burden must be linked in order to identify the requisite substantial burden:

> [T]he connection between the families' religious objections and the contraceptive coverage requirement is too attenuated to rank as substantial. The requirement carries no command that Hobby Lobby or Conestoga purchase or provide the contraceptives they find objectionable. ... Importantly, the decisions whether to claim benefits under the plans are made not by Hobby Lobby or Conestoga, but by the covered employees and dependents, in consultation with their health care providers. ... Any decision to use contraceptives made by a woman covered under Hobby Lobby's or Conestoga's plan will not be propelled by the Government, it will be the woman's autonomous choice, informed by the physician she consults.[29]

The dissent emphasized that the "linkage" between the burden imposed by the government's mandate and the religious beliefs offended by the mandate would be "interrupted by independent decisionmakers (the woman and her health counselor)" in a manner that would undermine characterization of the burden imposed by the government as "substantial."[30]

Compelling Interest

The Court's analysis of the government's interest in requiring contraceptive coverage appeared skeptical, but ultimately it assumed that the interests were sufficiently compelling.[31] The majority noted that the government's justifications—public health and gender equality—were too broadly defined, explaining that RFRA requires a "'more focused' inquiry."[32] It cited a 2006 case in which the Court held that, under RFRA, the government must demonstrate a compelling interest for prohibiting an exemption for a religious purpose while allowing exemptions for other purposes.[33] The majority's discussion suggested that the stated interests were undermined by the extent of other businesses that were exempt from offering their employees coverage (e.g., grandfathered plans, employers with fewer than 50 employees).[34]

Though the Court noted its concern regarding the sufficiency of the government's asserted interest, it conceded the compelling interest prong of the RFRA analysis with little discussion. However, the dissent addressed the compelling interest in greater detail, responding to the majority's concern about other exemptions undermining the government's alleged interest by citing a number of other federal laws that include exemptions for small employers without undermining the statutory interests.[35]

Least Restrictive Means

The Court rejected HHS's argument that it lacked other means to ensure availability of contraceptive coverage without burdening these companies' religious exercise, noting a few alternatives it considered "less restrictive."[36] First, the majority suggested that "[t]he most straightforward way ... would be for the Government to assume the cost of providing" coverage to women whose employers object to providing coverage.[37] Second, the Court highlighted the availability of the accommodation already established for nonprofit employers with religious objections, which would "protect the asserted needs of women as effectively" as the contraceptive coverage requirement without "requiring employers to fund contraceptive methods that violate their religious beliefs."[38] Though the Court cited the accommodation as one potential less restrictive alternative, it explicitly noted that it was not determining its sufficiency under RFRA for the purpose of any other legal challenge.[39] Discussed in further detail later in this report, the accommodation currently is available to certain nonprofit religious organizations who self-certify their objection to qualify as eligible to have the insurance issuer provide coverage to the employees outside of the employer's group health plan.

In response to these alternatives, the dissent questioned the extent to which the majority would allow employers with religious objections to government mandates to avoid compliance:

> And where is the stopping point to the "let the government pay" alternative? Suppose an employer's sincerely held religious belief is offended by health coverage of vaccines, or paying the minimum wage, or according women equal pay for substantially similar work? Does it rank as a less restrictive alternative to require the government to provide the money or benefit to which the employer has a religion-based objection?[40]

According to the majority, the dissent's concern with the potential assumption of costs by the government for private objections to various legal requirements was unfounded because its decision reached only to the contraceptive coverage requirement.[41] It explained that its decision should not be interpreted to mean that insurance coverage mandates generally cannot be upheld if they conflict with an employer's religious beliefs.[42] The majority stated that "[o]ther coverage requirements, such as immunizations, may be supported by different interests ... and may involve different arguments about the least restrictive means of providing them."[43]

SELECTED POTENTIAL LEGISLATIVE RESPONSES FOLLOWING *HOBBY LOBBY*

A number of potential legislative responses have been mentioned since the Court announced its decision in *Hobby Lobby*. It is important to remember that the Court's decision was based on the statutory protections in RFRA, not in constitutional protections of the First Amendment. Just as Congress may enact heightened protections for religious exercise as it did in RFRA and as it may determine the scope of protection available, it may enact statutory language to clarify the effect of RFRA regardless of the Court's decision. The Court essentially created a working definition of person under RFRA, but Congress may confirm or alter that definition at its discretion. Alternatively, it may consider preempting RFRA with respect to certain legislative requirements.

Amending RFRA to Clarify the Scope of Applicability

The most direct congressional response to *Hobby Lobby* would be to amend RFRA to include a definition of *person* and in effect clarify the scope of RFRA's applicability generally. This legislative option creates a number of possibilities, ranging from a definition of person to include only natural persons at one end to a definition that includes all natural and artificial persons at the other end, similar to the definition provided under the Dictionary Act used by the Court.

Aside from these two extreme ends of the spectrum, Congress may consider a number of intermediate definitions. The working definition resulting from the Court's decision in *Hobby Lobby* has been considered as one type of compromise between eliminating protection for any corporations and extending protection for all corporations. Although not necessary in light of the decision, Congress may choose to adopt explicitly the Court's definition to avoid any future cases from expanding or restricting the status quo following *Hobby Lobby*.

Alternatively, Congress may consider other examples when considering the scope of "persons" to which it wants RFRA to apply. The preeminent example of Congress's provision of protection for potential religious objectors from a generally applicable mandate is Title VII of the Civil Rights Act of 1964. Title VII, in part, prohibits employers from discriminating against employees on the basis of their religious beliefs.[44] Because this provision may interfere with religious employers' religious practices (e.g., hiring employees of the same faith of the organization), Congress included an exemption for religious entities, stating that the prohibition against religious discrimination does not apply to "a religious corporation, association, educational institution, or society with respect to the employment of individuals of a particular religion...."[45] This provision explicitly applies only to religious organizations, and courts generally have interpreted the scope of the provision to take into account (1) the purpose or mission of the organization; (2) the ownership, affiliation, or financial support of the organization; (3) requirements placed upon staff and members of the organization; and (4) the extent of religious practices in or the religious nature of the products and services offered by the organization and whether it operates for a profit.[46] A definition of person that would include language similar to Title VII likely would cover religious nonprofit organizations (e.g., charities, hospitals, schools), but would not cover commercial entities like Hobby Lobby.[47]

Preempting RFRA

Another option that may be used in response to *Hobby Lobby* would be to consider preempting RFRA in federal legislation. Under the legal principle of entrenchment, a legislative action in one Congress cannot bind a future Congress. That is, Congress cannot entrench a legislative action by providing that it may not be repealed or altered.[48] Accordingly, Congress may decide to enact legislation that would make RFRA not applicable to certain federal actions. For example, if Congress determined that it did not want to extend heightened protection that is otherwise provided under RFRA in certain instances (e.g., the contraceptive coverage mandate), it could enact a provision in the relevant legislation indicating that RFRA would not apply. Unlike the previous potential legislative response, this approach would mean that Congress considers RFRA's applicability to each present and future law on a case-by-case basis.

Shortly after *Hobby Lobby* was announced, the House and Senate introduced legislation that used this approach.[49] The Protect Women's Health From Corporate Interference Act of 2014 prohibited employers from denying coverage of any health care services required to be covered under federal law or regulation.[50] However, to prevent employers from claiming exemption under RFRA, the bill stated that the prohibition "shall apply notwithstanding any other provision of Federal law, including [RFRA]."[51] Accordingly, to the extent that a party may be covered by RFRA as a general matter, such parties would not be protected from coverage requirements imposed by federal law or regulation if the bill were enacted.

Effect on Contraceptive Coverage Requirements

Hobby Lobby expanded protection under RFRA to closely held corporations and held that such companies could not be required to include contraceptive coverage in their group health plans to the extent that they objected to contraceptives based on their religious beliefs. The Court did not decide the legal issues related to the religious exemption and accommodation available for churches and religious organizations, nor did it address protection from state requirements. As a result, a number of legal questions remain with regard to the obligations of employers to provide contraceptive coverage.

Current Protection for Religious Nonprofit Organizations

Since ACA's enactment, HHS has developed various iterations of administrative regulations to address religious objections to ACA's contraceptive coverage requirement and promulgated final rules in July 2013.[52] These rules respond to religious entities' objections to contraceptive coverage in two ways: (1) an exemption for religious employers covered under subsections (a)(1), (a)(3)(A)(i), or (a)(3)(A)(iii) of Section 6033 of the tax code and (2) an accommodation for other eligible organizations.[53]

Entities covered by the relevant provisions for the exemption generally include churches, church auxiliaries, church associations, or other religious orders.[54] Under the exemption, employees of religious employers would not receive contraceptive coverage either from their employer or from the issuer directly.

Employers that are not covered by the exemption may instead seek protection through the accommodation. To qualify for the accommodation, an organization must (1) object to coverage of at least some of the contraceptive services based on religious beliefs; (2) be a nonprofit entity; (3) hold itself out as a religious organization; and (4) comply with the self-certification requirements of the rule.[55] Under the accommodation, employees of eligible organizations would not receive contraceptive coverage from their employer, but would have coverage provided directly through the health plan issuer at no cost to the employee or the employer.

These regulations remain in effect and were not at issue in *Hobby Lobby*. Thus, churches and religious nonprofit organizations may still avoid penalties for noncompliance. However, some of the organizations that would qualify for protection under the regulations have challenged the contraceptive coverage mandate separately, claiming that the certification process for the accommodation burdens their religious exercise.[56] These cases are not directly related to the decision in *Hobby Lobby*, though the Court's opinion has been cited by some to suggest that the accommodation would be upheld if such a case reached the Court. [57]

Notably, three days after the *Hobby Lobby* decision was announced, the Court issued an injunction effectively preventing enforcement of the contraceptive coverage requirement against Wheaton College pending a final decision in its case if the school provided written notice to HHS of its qualifications for the accommodation.[58] Providing such a letter would allow the school to claim eligibility without using the official form—to which they object—prescribed by the regulations. Although the order explicitly emphasized that it was not "an expression of the Court's views on the merits" of the case, three Justices wrote in dissent from the Court's order.[59] The dissenting Justices stated that the college's assertion "that its filing of a self-certification form will make it complicit in the provision of contraceptives by triggering the obligation for someone else to provide the services to which it objects" was not a viable claim under RFRA and therefore not eligible for injunctive relief.[60] The dissenters noted that the *Hobby Lobby* decision considered the accommodation to be "'an alternative that achieves all of the Government's aims while providing greater respect for religious liberty.'"[61] Despite the widespread attention being paid to the *Wheaton* order, it indeed does not provide any final decision on the merits of the challenge to the accommodation. Additionally, though the majority in *Hobby Lobby* noted the possibility that the accommodation could be a "less restrictive" means to achieve the government's interest in the contraceptive coverage mandate, it did not determine it to be the *least* restrictive means.[62] In other words, simply because the Court pointed to the accommodation as an option that burdened the companies' religious exercise less does not mean that there may not be a third option that minimized the burden even more effectively.

State Coverage Requirements

Hobby Lobby involved a challenge to the federal contraceptive coverage requirement by companies seeking protection under the federal RFRA. Thus, the decision to expand protection under RFRA to closely held corporations affects only federal law. A number of states have enacted separate contraceptive coverage requirements, predating the ACA.[63] Therefore, the closely held companies that now have been recognized as covered by RFRA may still be obligated to provide contraceptive coverage under state legal requirements if the states do not have an applicable exemption to such coverage requirements.

Such companies may seek protection under state versions of RFRA, as the federal RFRA only applies to protect against burdens imposed by federal actions. Many states enacted laws which may be modeled on the federal RFRA to prohibit state governments from substantially burdening religious exercise. The applicability of these state RFRAs to various types of organizations would depend on each state's legislative language. If the state RFRA did not define the entities which may claim protection, a court may look to *Hobby Lobby* as guidance in interpreting the proper scope, but would not be bound to reach the same conclusion as the Court did.

End Notes

[1] Patient Protection and Affordable Care Act, P.L. 111-148, § 1001(5), 111th Cong., 2nd Sess. (2010).

[2] Burwell v. Hobby Lobby Stores, Inc., Nos. 13-354 and 13-356, 2014 U.S. LEXIS 4505 (U.S. 2014).

[3] P.L. 103-141, codified at 42 U.S.C. § 2000bb et seq.

[4] 128 S.Ct. 1471 (2008).

[5] U.S. Const. amend. I.

[6] *See* Sherbert v. Verner, 374 U.S. 398 (1963); Wisconsin v. Yoder, 406 U.S. 205 (1972).

[7] Employment Division, Department of Human Resources of Oregon v. Smith, 494 U.S. 872, 879 (1990) (internal quotes omitted).

[8] *Id.* at 890.

[9] 42 U.S.C. § 2000bb-1.

[10] 42 U.S.C. § 2000bb-1(b).

[11] *Hobby Lobby*, 2014 U.S. LEXIS 4505 at *40-*42.

[12] *See* 1 U.S.C. § 1.

[13] *Hobby Lobby*, 2014 U.S. LEXIS 4505 at *13.

[14] *Id.* at *38-*42.

[15] *Id.* at *118 (Ginsburg, J., dissenting) ("Until this litigation, no decision of this Court recognized a for-profit corporation's qualification for a religious exemption from a generally applicable law, whether under the Free Exercise Clause or RFRA. The absence of such precedent is just what one would expect, for the exercise of religion is characteristic of natural persons, not artificial legal entities.")

[16] *See* Braunfeld v. Brown, 366 U.S. 599 (1961).

[17] *See* Corp. of Presiding Bishop of Church of Jesus Christ of Latter-Day Saints v. Amos, 483 U.S. 327 (1987); Church of the Lukumi Babalu Aye, Inc. v. Hialeah, 508 U.S. 520 (1993); Gonzales v. o Centro Espirita Beneficiente Uniao do Vegetal, 546 U.S. 418 (2006); Hosanna-Tabor Evangelical Lutheran Church and School v. EEOC, 132 S.Ct. 694 (2012).

[18] *Hobby Lobby*, 2014 U.S. LEXIS 4505 at *43-*44.
[19] *Id.* at *58.
[20] *Id.*
[21] *Id.*
[22] *Id.* at *97.
[23] *Id.* at *128.
[24] *Id.* at *63.
[25] *Id.* at *64.
[26] *Id.* at *63-*64 ("If the companies continue to offer group health plans that do not cover the contraceptives at issue, they will be taxed $100 per day for each affected individual.").
[27] *Id.* at *64. Under ACA, if companies stop providing "insurance coverage altogether and thus forc[e] their employees to obtain health insurance on one of the exchanges established under ACA" and one or more full-time employees "were to qualify for a subsidy on one of the government-run exchanges, ... [t]he companies could face penalties of $2,000 per employee each year." *Id.*
[28] *Id.* at *133-*134.
[29] *Id.* at *134-*135.
[30] *Id.* at *135.
[31] *Id.* at *76-*77.
[32] *Id.* at *74 (quoting *O Centro*, 546 U.S. at 430-31).
[33] *Id.* at *74-*75.
[34] *Id.* at *76.
[35] *Id.* at *139-*141.
[36] Id. at *77-82.
[37] *Id.* at *77.
[38] *Id.* at *82-*83.
[39] *Id.* at *83.
[40] *Id.* at *144-*145 (internal citations omitted).
[41] *Id.* at *86.
[42] *Id.* at *86-*87.
[43] *Id.* at *87.
[44] 42 U.S.C. § 2000e-2. *See also* 42 U.S.C. § 2000e(j).
[45] 42 U.S.C. § 2000e-1(a).
[46] *See, e.g.*, LeBoon v. Lancaster County Jewish Community Center Association, 503 F.3d 217, 226-27 (3rd Cir. 2007) (providing summary discussion of the circuit courts' interpretations of which organizations qualify for exemption under Title VII).
[47] *See* Equal Employment Opportunity Commission v. Townley Engineering & Manufacturing Co., 859 F.2d 610 (9th Cir. 1988).
[48] *See* Fletcher v. Peck, 10 U.S. 87, 135 (Chief Justice Marshall) ("The principle asserted is, that one legislature is competent to repeal any act which a former legislature was competent to pass; and that one legislature cannot abridge the powers of a succeeding legislature."). The Supreme Court has noted the long history of this rule. *See* United States v. Winstar Corp., 518 U.S. 839, 872-74 (1996).
[49] H.R. 5051/S. 2578, 113th Cong. (2014).
[50] *Id.* at § 4(a).
[51] *Id.* at § 4(b).
[52] *See* CRS Report WSLG689, *History and Current Status for Enforcement of ACA's Contraceptive Coverage Requirement.*

[53] Coverage of Certain Preventive Health Services Under the Affordable Care Act, 78 Fed. Reg. 39,870 (July 2, 2013).

[54] *See* 26 U.S.C. § 6033(a)(3)(A)(i), (iii).

[55] *See* 45 C.F.R. § 147.131(b).

[56] *See* Wheaton College v. Burwell, No. 13A1284 (U.S. July 3, 2014); Little Sisters of the Poor v. Sebelius, No. 13A691 (U.S. Jan. 24, 2014).

[57] Jess Bravin, *Administration Points to Hobby Lobby Ruling in Wheaton College Case*, WALL STREET JOURNAL (July 2, 2014) (noting that U.S. Solicitor General Donald Verrilli argued that the Court's decision in Hobby Lobby indicated that the accommodation was not improper under RFRA).

[58] Wheaton College v. Burwell, No. 13A1284 (U.S. July 3, 2014).

[59] *Id.* at 2.

[60] *Id.* at 3.

[61] *Id.* ("After expressly relying on the availability of the religious-nonprofit accommodation to hold that the contraceptive coverage requirement violates RFRA as applied to closely held for-profit corporations, the Court now, as the dissent in Hobby Lobby feared it might, retreats from that position." (citations omitted)).

[62] *See Hobby Lobby*, 2014 U.S. LEXIS 4505 at *82 ("We do not decide today whether an approach [of the accommodation] complies with RFRA for purposes of all religious claims.").

[63] *See State Policies in Brief: Insurance Coverage of Contraceptives*, Guttmacher Institute (July 2, 2014), *available at* http://www.guttmacher.org/statecenter/spibs/spib_ICC

In: Free Exercise
Editor: Aubrey Boone

ISBN: 978-1-61122-062-9

Chapter 2

DECISION OF THE SUPREME COURT OF THE UNITED STATES IN THE CASE OF BURWELL, SECRETARY OF HEALTH AND HUMAN SERVICES ET AL. V. HOBBY LOBBY STORES, INC., ET AL.*

Note: Where it is feasible, a syllabus (headnote) will be released, as is being done in connection with this case, at the time the opinion is issued. The syllabus constitutes no part of the opinion of the Court but has been prepared by the Reporter of Decisions for the convenience of the reader. See *United States* v. *Detroit Timber & Lumber Co.,* 200 U. S. 321, 337.

CERTIORARI TO THE UNITED STATES COURT OF APPEALS FOR THE TENTH CIRCUIT

No. 13–354. Argued March 25, 2014—Decided June 30, 2014**

The Religious Freedom Restoration Act of 1993 (RFRA) prohibits the "Government [from] substantially burden[ing] a person's exercise of religion even if the burden results from a rule of general applicability" unless the

* This is an edited, reformatted and augmented version of the official slip opinion as delivered by the U.S. Supreme Court on June 30, 2014.

** Together with No. 13–356, *Conestoga Wood Specialties Corp. et al.* v. *Burwell, Secretary of Health and Human Services, et al.,* on certiorari to the United States Court of Appeals for the Third Circuit.

Government "demonstrates that application of the burden to the person—(1) is in furtherance of a compelling governmental interest; and (2) is the least restrictive means of furthering that compelling governmental interest." 42 U. S. C. §§2000bb–1(a), (b). As amended by the Religious Land Use and Institutionalized Persons Act of 2000 (RLUIPA), RFRA covers "any exercise of religion, whether or not compelled by, or central to, a system of religious belief." §2000cc–5(7)(A).

At issue here are regulations promulgated by the Department of Health and Human Services (HHS) under the Patient Protection and Affordable Care Act of 2010 (ACA), which, as relevant here, requires specified employers' group health plans to furnish "preventive care and screenings" for women without "any cost sharing requirements," 42 U. S. C. §300gg–13(a)(4). Congress did not specify what types of preventive care must be covered; it authorized the Health Resources and Services Administration, a component of HHS, to decide. *Ibid.* Nonexempt employers are generally required to provide coverage for the 20 contraceptive methods approved by the Food and Drug Administration, including the 4 that may have the effect of preventing an already fertilized egg from developing any further by inhibiting its attachment to the uterus. Religious employers, such as churches, are exempt from this contraceptive mandate. HHS has also effectively exempted religious nonprofit organizations with religious objections to providing coverage for contraceptive services. Under this accommodation, the insurance issuer must exclude contraceptive coverage from the employer's plan and provide plan participants with separate payments for contraceptive services without imposing any cost-sharing requirements on the employer, its insurance plan, or its employee beneficiaries.

In these cases, the owners of three closely held for-profit corporations have sincere Christian beliefs that life begins at conception and that it would violate their religion to facilitate access to contraceptive drugs or devices that operate after that point. In separate actions, they sued HHS and other federal officials and agencies (collectively HHS) under RFRA and the Free Exercise Clause, seeking to enjoin application of the contraceptive mandate insofar as it requires them to provide health coverage for the four objectionable contraceptives. In No. 13–356, the District Court denied the Hahns and their company—Conestoga Wood Specialties—a preliminary injunction. Affirming, the Third Circuit held that a for-profit corporation could not "engage in religious exercise" under RFRA or the First Amendment, and that the mandate imposed no requirements on the Hahns in their personal capacity. In No. 13–354, the Greens, their children, and their companies—Hobby Lobby Stores and Mardel—were also denied a preliminary injunction, but the Tenth Circuit reversed. It held that the Greens' businesses are "persons" under RFRA, and that the corporations had established a likelihood of success on their RFRA claim because the contraceptive mandate substantially burdened their exercise of religion and HHS had not demonstrated a compelling interest in enforcing the mandate against them; in the alternative, the court held that HHS had not proved that the mandate was the "least restrictive means" of furthering a compelling governmental interest.

Held: As applied to closely held corporations, the HHS regulations imposing the contraceptive mandate violate RFRA. Pp. 16–49.

(a) RFRA applies to regulations that govern the activities of closely held for-profit corporations like Conestoga, Hobby Lobby, and Mardel. Pp. 16–31.

(1) HHS argues that the companies cannot sue because they are for-profit corporations, and that the owners cannot sue because the regulations apply only to the companies, but that would leave merchants with a difficult choice: give up the right to seek judicial protection of their religious liberty or forgo the benefits of operating as corporations. RFRA's text shows that Congress designed the statute to provide very broad protection for religious liberty and did not intend to put merchants to such a choice. It employed the familiar legal fiction of including corporations within RFRA's definition of "persons," but the purpose of extending rights to corporations is to protect the rights of people associated with the corporation, including shareholders, officers, and employees. Protecting the free-exercise rights of closely held corporations thus protects the religious liberty of the humans who own and control them. Pp. 16–19.

(2) HHS and the dissent make several unpersuasive arguments. Pp. 19–31.

(i) Nothing in RFRA suggests a congressional intent to depart from the Dictionary Act definition of "person," which "include[s] corporations, . . . as well as individuals." 1 U. S. C. §1. The Court has entertained RFRA and free-exercise claims brought by nonprofit corporations. See, *e.g., Gonzales* v. *O Centro Espírita Beneficiente União do Vegetal*, 546 U. S. 418. And HHS's concession that a nonprofit corporation can be a "person" under RFRA effectively dispatches any argument that the term does not reach for-profit corporations; no conceivable definition of "person" includes natural persons and non-profit corporations, but not for-profit corporations. Pp. 19–20.

(ii) HHS and the dissent nonetheless argue that RFRA does not cover Conestoga, Hobby Lobby, and Mardel because they cannot "exercise . . . religion." They offer no persuasive explanation for this conclusion. The corporate form alone cannot explain it because RFRA indisputably protects nonprofit corporations. And the profit-making objective of the corporations cannot explain it because the Court has entertained the free-exercise claims of individuals who were attempting to make a profit as retail merchants. *Braunfeld* v. *Brown*, 366 U. S. 599. Business practices compelled or limited by the tenets of a religious doctrine fall comfortably within the understanding of the "exercise of religion" that this Court set out in *Employment Div., Dept. of Human Resources of Ore.* v. *Smith*, 494 U. S. 872, 877. Any suggestion that for-profit corporations are incapable of exercising religion because their purpose is simply to make money flies in the face of modern corporate law. States, including those in which the plaintiff corporations were incorporated, authorize corporations to pursue any lawful purpose or business, including the pursuit of profit in conformity with the owners' religious principles. Pp. 20–25.

(iii) Also flawed is the claim that RFRA offers no protection because it only codified pre-*Smith* Free Exercise Clause precedents, none of which squarely recognized free-exercise rights for for-profit corporations. First, nothing in RFRA as originally enacted suggested that its definition of "exercise of religion" was meant to be tied to pre-*Smith* interpretations of the First Amendment. Second, if RFRA's original text were not clear enough, the RLUIPA amendment surely dispels any doubt that Congress intended to separate the definition of the phrase from that in First Amendment case law. Third, the pre-*Smith* case of *Gallagher* v. *Crown Kosher Super Market of Mass., Inc.*, 366 U. S. 617, suggests, if anything, that for-profit corporations can exercise religion. Finally, the results would be absurd if RFRA, a law enacted to provide very broad protection for religious liberty, merely restored this Court's pre-*Smith* decisions in ossified form and restricted RFRA claims to plaintiffs who fell within a category of plaintiffs whose claims the Court had recognized before *Smith*. Pp. 25–28.

(3) Finally, HHS contends that Congress could not have wanted RFRA to apply to for-profit corporations because of the difficulty of ascertaining the "beliefs" of large, publicly traded corporations, but HHS has not pointed to any example of a publicly traded corporation asserting RFRA rights, and numerous practical restraints would likely prevent that from occurring. HHS has also provided no evidence that the purported problem of determining the sincerity of an asserted religious belief moved Congress to exclude for-profit corporations from RFRA's protection. That disputes among the owners of corporations might arise is not a problem unique to this context. State corporate law provides a ready means for resolving any conflicts by, for example, dictating how a corporation can establish its governing structure. Courts will turn to that structure and the underlying state law in resolving disputes. Pp. 29–31.

(b) HHS's contraceptive mandate substantially burdens the exercise of religion. Pp. 31–38.

(1) It requires the Hahns and Greens to engage in conduct that seriously violates their sincere religious belief that life begins at conception. If they and their companies refuse to provide contraceptive coverage, they face severe economic consequences: about $475 million per year for Hobby Lobby, $33 million per year for Conestoga, and $15 million per year for Mardel. And if they drop coverage altogether, they could face penalties of roughly $26 million for Hobby Lobby, $1.8 million for Conestoga, and $800,000 for Mardel. P. 32.

(2) *Amici* supporting HHS argue that the $2,000 per-employee penalty is less than the average cost of providing insurance, and therefore that dropping insurance coverage eliminates any substantial burden imposed by the mandate. HHS has never argued this and the Court does not know its position with respect to the argument. But even if the Court reached the argument, it would find it unpersuasive: It ignores the fact that the plaintiffs

have religious reasons for providing health-insurance coverage for their employees, and it is far from clear that the net cost to the companies of providing insurance is more than the cost of dropping their insurance plans and paying the ACA penalty. Pp. 32–35.

(3) HHS argues that the connection between what the objecting parties must do and the end that they find to be morally wrong is too attenuated because it is the employee who will choose the coverage and contraceptive method she uses. But RFRA's question is whether the mandate imposes a substantial burden on the objecting parties' ability to conduct business in accordance with *their religious beliefs.* The belief of the Hahns and Greens implicates a difficult and important question of religion and moral philosophy, namely, the circumstances under which it is immoral for a person to perform an act that is innocent in itself but that has the effect of enabling or facilitating the commission of an immoral act by another. It is not for the Court to say that the religious beliefs of the plaintiffs are mistaken or unreasonable. In fact, this Court considered and rejected a nearly identical argument in *Thomas* v. *Review Bd. of Indiana Employment Security Div.*, 450 U. S. 707. The Court's "narrow function . . . is to determine" whether the plaintiffs' asserted religious belief reflects "an honest conviction," *id.*, at 716, and there is no dispute here that it does. *Tilton* v. *Richardson*, 403 U. S. 672, 689; and *Board of Ed. Of Central School Dist. No. 1* v. *Allen*, 392 U. S. 236, 248–249, distinguished. Pp. 35–38.

(c) The Court assumes that the interest in guaranteeing cost-free access to the four challenged contraceptive methods is a compelling governmental interest, but the Government has failed to show that the contraceptive mandate is the least restrictive means of furthering that interest. Pp. 38–49.

(1) The Court assumes that the interest in guaranteeing cost-free access to the four challenged contraceptive methods is compelling within the meaning of RFRA. Pp. 39–40.

(2) The Government has failed to satisfy RFRA's least-restrictive-means standard. HHS has not shown that it lacks other means of achieving its desired goal without imposing a substantial burden on the exercise of religion. The Government could, *e.g.*, assume the cost of providing the four contraceptives to women unable to

obtain coverage due to their employers' religious objections. Or it could extend the accommodation that HHS has already established for religious nonprofit organizations to non-profit employers with religious objections to the contraceptive mandate. That accommodation does not impinge on the plaintiffs' religious beliefs that providing insurance coverage for the contraceptives at issue here violates their religion and it still serves HHS's stated interests. Pp. 40–45.

(3) This decision concerns only the contraceptive mandate and should not be understood to hold that all insurance-coverage mandates, *e.g.,* for vaccinations or blood transfusions, must necessarily fall if they conflict with an employer's religious beliefs. Nor does it provide a shield for employers who might cloak illegal discrimination as a religious practice. *United States* v. *Lee*, 455 U. S. 252, which up-held the payment of Social Security taxes despite an employer's religious objection, is not analogous. It turned primarily on the special problems associated with a national system of taxation; and if *Lee* were a RFRA case, the fundamental point would still be that there is no less restrictive alternative to the categorical requirement to pay taxes. Here, there is an alternative to the contraceptive mandate. Pp. 45–49.

No. 13–354, 723 F. 3d 1114, affirmed; No. 13–356, 724 F. 3d 377, reversed and remanded.

ALITO, J., delivered the opinion of the Court, in which ROBERTS, C. J., and SCALIA, KENNEDY, and THOMAS, JJ., joined. KENNEDY, J., filed a concurring opinion. GINSBURG, J., filed a dissenting opinion, in which SOTOMAYOR, J., joined, and in which BREYER and KAGAN, JJ., joined as to all but Part III–C–1. BREYER and KAGAN, JJ., filed a dissenting opinion.

Opinion of the Court

NOTICE: This opinion is subject to formal revision before publication in thepreliminary print of the United States Reports. Readers are requested tonotify the Reporter of Decisions, Supreme Court of the United States, Washington, D.C. 20543, of any typographical or other formal errors, in orderthat corrections may be made before the preliminary print goes to press.

Nos. 13–354 and 13–356

Sylvia Burwell, Secretary of Health and Human Services, et al.,
Petitioners

13–354 *v.*

Hobby Lobby Stores, Inc., et al.

On Writ of Certiorari to the United States Court of Appeals for the
Tenth Circuit
and

Conestoga Wood Specialties Corporation et al., Petitioners

13–356 *v.*

Sylvia Burwell, Secretary of Health and Human Services, et al.

On Writ of Certiorari to the United States Court of Appeals for the
Third Circuit
[June 30, 2014]

JUSTICE ALITO delivered the opinion of the Court.

We must decide in these cases whether the Religious Freedom Restoration Act of 1993 (RFRA), 107 Stat. 1488, 42 U. S. C. §2000bb *et seq.*, permits the United States Department of Health and Human Services (HHS) to demand that three closely held corporations provide health-insurance coverage for methods of contraception that violate the sincerely held religious beliefs of the companies' owners. We hold that the regulations that impose this obligation violate RFRA, which prohibits the Federal Government from taking any action that substantially burdens the exercise of religion unless that action constitutes the least restrictive means of serving a compelling government interest.

In holding that the HHS mandate is unlawful, we reject HHS's argument that the owners of the companies forfeited all RFRA protection when they decided to organize their businesses as corporations rather than sole proprietorships or general partnerships. The plain terms of RFRA make it perfectly clear that Congress did not discriminate in this way against men and women who wish to run their businesses as for-profit corporations in the manner required by their religious beliefs.

Since RFRA applies in these cases, we must decide whether the challenged HHS regulations substantially burden the exercise of religion, and we hold that they do. The owners of the businesses have religious objections to abortion, and according to their religious beliefs the four contraceptive methods at issue are abortifacients. If the owners comply with the HHS mandate, they believe they will be facilitating abortions, and if they do not comply, they will pay a very heavy price—as much as $1.3 million per day, or about $475 million per year, in the case of one of the companies. If these consequences do not amount to a substantial burden, it is hard to see what would.

Under RFRA, a Government action that imposes a substantial burden on religious exercise must serve a compelling government interest, and we assume that the HHS regulations satisfy this requirement. But in order for the HHS mandate to be sustained, it must also constitute the least restrictive means of serving that interest, and the mandate plainly fails that test. There are other ways in which Congress or HHS could equally ensure that every woman has cost-free access to the particular contraceptives at issue here and, indeed, to all FDA-approved contraceptives.

In fact, HHS has already devised and implemented a system that seeks to respect the religious liberty of religious nonprofit corporations while ensuring that the employees of these entities have precisely the same access to all FDA-approved contraceptives as employees of companies whose owners have no religious objections to providing such coverage. The employees of these religious nonprofit corporations still have access to insurance coverage without cost sharing for all FDA-approved contraceptives; and according to HHS, this system imposes no net economic burden on the insurance companies that are required to provide or secure the coverage.

Although HHS has made this system available to religious nonprofits that have religious objections to the contraceptive mandate, HHS has provided no reason why the same system cannot be made available when the owners of for-profit corporations have similar religious objections. We therefore conclude that this system constitutes an alternative that achieves all of the Government's aims while providing greater respect for religious liberty. And under RFRA, that conclusion means that enforcement of the HHS contraceptive mandate against the objecting parties in these cases is unlawful.

As this description of our reasoning shows, our holding is very specific. We do not hold, as the principal dissent alleges, that for-profit corporations and other commercial enterprises can "opt out of any law (saving only tax laws) they judge incompatible with their sincerely held religious beliefs." *Post*, at 1 (opinion of GINSBURG, J.). Nor do we hold, as the dissent implies, that such corporations have free rein to take steps that impose "disadvantages . . . on others" or that require "the general public [to] pick up the tab." *Post*, at 1–2. And we certainly do not hold or suggest that "RFRA demands accommodation of a for-profit corporation's religious beliefs no matter the impact that accommodation may have on . . . thousands of women employed by Hobby Lobby." *Post,* at 2.[1] The effect of the HHS-created accommodation on the women employed by Hobby Lobby and the other companies involved in these cases would be precisely zero. Under that accommodation, these women would still be entitled to all FDA-approved contraceptives without cost sharing.

I

A

Congress enacted RFRA in 1993 in order to provide very broad protection for religious liberty. RFRA's enactment came three years after this Court's decision in *Employ ment Div., Dept. of Human Resources of Ore.* v. *Smith*, 494 U. S. 872 (1990), which largely repudiated the method of analyzing free-exercise claims that had been used in cases like *Sherbert* v. *Verner*, 374 U. S. 398 (1963), and *Wiscon sin* v. *Yoder*, 406 U. S. 205 (1972). In determining whether challenged government actions violated the Free Exercise Clause of the First Amendment, those decisions used a balancing test that took into account whether the challenged action imposed a substantial burden on the practice of religion, and if it did, whether it was needed to serve a compelling government interest. Applying this test, the Court held in *Sherbert* that an employee who was fired for refusing to work on her Sabbath could not be denied unemployment benefits. 374 U. S., at 408–409. And in *Yoder,* the Court held that Amish children could not be required to comply with a state law demanding that they remain in school until the age of 16 even though their religion required them to focus on uniquely Amish values and beliefs during their formative adolescent years. 406 U. S., at 210–211, 234–236.

In *Smith,* however, the Court rejected "the balancing test set forth in *Sherbert.*" 494 U. S., at 883. *Smith* concerned two members of the Native American Church who were fired for ingesting peyote for sacramental purposes. When they sought unemployment benefits, the State of Oregon rejected their claims on the ground that consumption of peyote was a crime, but the Oregon Supreme Court, applying the *Sherbert* test, held that the denial of benefits violated the Free Exercise Clause. 494 U. S., at 875.

This Court then reversed, observing that use of the *Sherbert* test whenever a person objected on religious grounds to the enforcement of a generally applicable law "would open the prospect of constitutionally required religious exemptions from civic obligations of almost every conceivable kind." 494 U. S., at 888. The Court therefore held that, under the First Amendment, "neutral, generally applicable laws may be applied to religious practices even when not supported by a compelling governmental interest." *City of Boerne* v. *Flores*, 521 U. S. 507, 514 (1997).

Congress responded to *Smith* by enacting RFRA. "[L]aws [that are] 'neutral' toward religion," Congress found, "may burden religious exercise as surely as laws intended to interfere with religious exercise." 42 U. S. C. §2000bb(a)(2); see also §2000bb(a)(4). In order to ensure broad protection for religious liberty, RFRA provides that "Government shall not substantially burden a person's exercise of religion even if the burden results from a rule of general applicability." §2000bb–1(a).[2] If the Government substantially burdens a person's exercise of religion, under the Act that person is entitled to an exemption from the rule unless the Government "demonstrates that application of the burden to the person—(1) is in furtherance of a compelling governmental interest; and (2) is the least restrictive means of furthering that compelling governmental interest." §2000bb–1(b).[3]

As enacted in 1993, RFRA applied to both the Federal Government and the States, but the constitutional authority invoked for regulating federal and state agencies differed. As applied to a federal agency, RFRA is based on the enumerated power that supports the particular agency's work,[4] but in attempting to regulate the States and their subdivisions, Congress relied on its power under Section 5 of the Fourteenth Amendment to enforce the First Amendment. 521 U. S., at 516–517. In *City of Boerne*, however, we held that Congress had overstepped its Section 5 authority because "[t]he stringent test RFRA demands" "far exceed[ed] any pattern or practice of unconstitutional conduct under the Free Exercise Clause as interpreted in *Smith*." *Id.*, at 533–534. See also *id.*, at 532.

Following our decision in *City of Boerne*, Congress passed the Religious Land Use and Institutionalized Persons Act of 2000 (RLUIPA), 114 Stat. 803, 42 U. S. C. §2000cc *et seq*. That statute, enacted under Congress's Commerce and Spending Clause powers, imposes the same general test as RFRA but on a more limited category of governmental actions. See *Cutter* v. *Wilkinson*, 544 U. S. 709, 715–716 (2005). And, what is most relevant for present purposes, RLUIPA amended RFRA's definition of the "exercise of religion." See §2000bb–2(4) (importing RLUIPA definition). Before RLUIPA, RFRA's definition made reference to the First Amendment. See §2000bb–2(4) (1994 ed.) (defining "exercise of religion" as "the exercise of religion under the First Amendment"). In RLUIPA, in an obvious effort to effect a complete separation from First Amendment case law, Congress deleted the reference to the First Amendment and defined the "exercise of religion" to include "any exercise of religion, whether or not compelled by, or central to, a system of religious belief." §2000cc–5(7)(A). And Congress mandated that this concept "be construed in favor of a broad protection of religious exercise, to the maximum extent permitted by the terms of this chapter and the Constitution." §2000cc–3(g).[5]

B

At issue in these cases are HHS regulations promulgated under the Patient Protection and Affordable Care Act of 2010 (ACA), 124 Stat. 119. ACA generally requires employers with 50 or more full-time employees to offer "a group health plan or group health insurance coverage" that provides "minimum essential coverage." 26 U. S. C. §5000A(f)(2); §§4980H(a), (c)(2). Any covered employer that does not provide such coverage must pay a substantial price. Specifically, if a covered employer provides group health insurance but its plan fails to comply with ACA's group-health-plan requirements, the employer may be required to pay $100 per day for each affected "individual." §§4980D(a)–(b). And if the employer decides to stop providing health insurance altogether and at least one full-time employee enrolls in a health plan and qualifies for a subsidy on one of the government-run ACA exchanges, the employer must pay $2,000 per year for each of its fulltime employees. §§4980H(a), (c)(1).

Unless an exception applies, ACA requires an employer's group health plan or group-health-insurance coverage to furnish "preventive care and screenings" for women without "any cost sharing requirements." 42 U. S. C. §300gg–13(a)(4). Congress itself, however, did not specify what types of preventive care must be covered. Instead, Congress authorized the Health Resources and Services Administration (HRSA), a component of HHS, to make that important and sensitive decision. *Ibid.* The HRSA in turn consulted the Institute of Medicine, a nonprofit group of volunteer advisers, in determining which preventive services to require. See 77 Fed. Reg. 8725–8726 (2012).

In August 2011, based on the Institute's recommendations, the HRSA promulgated the Women's Preventive Services Guidelines. See *id.*, at 8725–8726, and n. 1; online at http://hrsa.gov/womensguidelines (all Internet materials as visited June 26, 2014, and available in Clerk of Court's case file). The Guidelines provide that nonexempt employers are generally required to provide "coverage, without cost sharing" for "[a]ll Food and Drug Administration [(FDA)] approved contraceptive methods, sterilization procedures, and patient education and counseling." 77 Fed. Reg. 8725 (internal quotation marks omitted). Although many of the required, FDA-approved methods of contraception work by preventing the fertilization of an egg, four of those methods (those specifically at issue in these cases) may have the effect of preventing an already fertilized egg from developing any further by inhibiting its attachment to the uterus. See Brief for HHS in No. 13–354, pp. 9–10, n. 4;[6] FDA, Birth Control: Medicines to Help You.[7]

HHS also authorized the HRSA to establish exemptions from the contraceptive mandate for "religious employers." 45 CFR §147.131(a). That category encompasses "churches, their integrated auxiliaries, and conventions or associations of churches," as well as "the exclusively religious activities of any religious order." See *ibid* (citing 26 U. S. C. §§6033(a)(3)(A)(i), (iii)). In its Guidelines, HRSA exempted these organizations from the requirement to cover contraceptive services. See http://hrsa.gov/womensguidelines.

In addition, HHS has effectively exempted certain religious nonprofit organizations, described under HHS regulations as "eligible organizations," from the contraceptive mandate. See 45 CFR §147.131(b); 78 Fed. Reg. 39874 (2013). An "eligible organization" means a nonprofit organization that "holds itself out as a religious organization" and "opposes providing coverage for some or all of any contraceptive services required to be covered . . . on account of religious objections." 45 CFR §147.131(b). To qualify for this accommodation, an employer must certify that it is such an organization. §147.131(b)(4). When a group-health-insurance issuer receives notice that one of its clients has invoked this provision, the issuer must then exclude contraceptive coverage from the employer's plan and provide separate payments for contraceptive services for plan participants without imposing any cost-sharing requirements on the eligible organization, its insurance plan, or its employee beneficiaries. §147.131(c).[8] Although this procedure requires the issuer to bear the cost of these services, HHS has determined that this obligation will not impose any net expense on issuers because its cost will be less than or equal to the cost savings resulting from the services. 78 Fed. Reg. 39877.[9]

In addition to these exemptions for religious organizations, ACA exempts a great many employers from most of its coverage requirements. Employers providing "grandfathered health plans"—those that existed prior to March 23,

2010, and that have not made specified changes after that date—need not comply with many of the Act's requirements, including the contraceptive mandate. 42 U. S. C. §§18011(a), (e). And employers with fewer than 50 employees are not required to provide health insurance at all. 26 U. S. C. §4980H(c)(2).

All told, the contraceptive mandate "presently does not apply to tens of millions of people." 723 F. 3d 1114, 1143 (CA10 2013). This is attributable, in large part, to grandfathered health plans: Over one-third of the 149 million nonelderly people in America with employer-sponsored health plans were enrolled in grandfathered plans in 2013. Brief for HHS in No. 13–354, at 53; Kaiser Family Foundation & Health Research & Educational Trust, Employer Health Benefits, 2013 Annual Survey 43, 221.[10] The count for employees working for firms that do not have to provide insurance at all because they employ fewer than 50 employees is 34 million workers. See The Whitehouse, Health Reform for Small Businesses: The Affordable Care Act Increases Choice and Saving Money for Small Businesses 1.[11]

II

A

Norman and Elizabeth Hahn and their three sons are devout members of the Mennonite Church, a Christian denomination. The Mennonite Church opposes abortion and believes that "[t]he fetus in its earliest stages . . . shares humanity with those who conceived it."[12]

Fifty years ago, Norman Hahn started a wood-working business in his garage, and since then, this company, Conestoga Wood Specialties, has grown and now has 950 employees. Conestoga is organized under Pennsylvania law as a for-profit corporation. The Hahns exercise sole ownership of the closely held business; they control its board of directors and hold all of its voting shares. One of the Hahn sons serves as the president and CEO.

The Hahns believe that they are required to run their business "in accordance with their religious beliefs and moral principles." 917 F. Supp. 2d 394, 402 (ED Pa. 2013). To that end, the company's mission, as they see it, is to "operate in a professional environment founded upon the highest ethical, moral, and Christian principles." *Ibid.* (internal quotation marks omitted). The company's "Vision and Values Statements" affirms that Conestoga endeavors to "ensur[e] a reasonable profit in [a] manner that reflects [the Hahns'] Christian heritage." App. in No. 13–356, p. 94 (complaint).

As explained in Conestoga's board-adopted "Statement on the Sanctity of Human Life," the Hahns believe that "human life begins at conception." 724

F. 3d 377, 382, and n. 5 (CA3 2013) (internal quotation marks omitted). It is therefore "against [their] moral conviction to be involved in the termination of human life" after conception, which they believe is a "sin against God to which they are held accountable." *Ibid.* (internal quotation marks omitted). The Hahns have accordingly excluded from the grouphealth-insurance plan they offer to their employees certain contraceptive methods that they consider to be abortifacients. *Id.*, at 382.

The Hahns and Conestoga sued HHS and other federal officials and agencies under RFRA and the Free Exercise Clause of the First Amendment, seeking to enjoin application of ACA's contraceptive mandate insofar as it requires them to provide health-insurance coverage for four FDAapproved contraceptives that may operate after the fertilization of an egg.[13] These include two forms of emergency contraception commonly called "morning after" pills and two types of intrauterine devices.[14]

In opposing the requirement to provide coverage for the contraceptives to which they object, the Hahns argued that "it is immoral and sinful for [them] to intentionally participate in, pay for, facilitate, or otherwise support these drugs." *Ibid.* The District Court denied a preliminary injunction, see 917 F. Supp. 2d, at 419, and the Third Circuit affirmed in a divided opinion, holding that "for-profit, secular corporations cannot engage in religious exercise" within the meaning of RFRA or the First Amendment. 724 F. 3d, at 381. The Third Circuit also rejected the claims brought by the Hahns themselves because it concluded that the HHS "[m]andate does not impose any requirements on the Hahns" in their personal capacity. *Id.*, at 389.

B

David and Barbara Green and their three children are Christians who own and operate two family businesses. Forty-five years ago, David Green started an arts-andcrafts store that has grown into a nationwide chain called Hobby Lobby. There are now 500 Hobby Lobby stores, and the company has more than 13,000 employees. 723 F. 3d, at 1122. Hobby Lobby is organized as a for-profit corporation under Oklahoma law.

One of David's sons started an affiliated business, Mardel, which operates 35 Christian bookstores and employs close to 400 people. *Ibid.* Mardel is also organized as a for-profit corporation under Oklahoma law.

Though these two businesses have expanded over the years, they remain closely held, and David, Barbara, and their children retain exclusive control of both companies. *Ibid.* David serves as the CEO of Hobby Lobby, and his three children serve as the president, vice president, and vice CEO. See Brief for Respondents in No. 13–354, p. 8.[15]

Hobby Lobby's statement of purpose commits the Greens to "[h]onoring the Lord in all [they] do by operating the company in a manner consistent with Biblical principles." App. in No. 13–354, pp. 134–135 (complaint). Each family member has signed a pledge to run the businesses in accordance with the family's religious beliefs and to use the family assets to support Christian ministries. 723 F. 3d, at 1122. In accordance with those commitments, Hobby Lobby and Mardel stores close on Sundays, even though the Greens calculate that they lose millions in sales annually by doing so. *Id.*, at 1122; App. in No. 13–354, at 136–137. The businesses refuse to engage in profitable transactions that facilitate or promote alcohol use; they contribute profits to Christian missionaries and ministries; and they buy hundreds of full-page newspaper ads inviting people to "know Jesus as Lord and Savior." *Ibid.* (internal quotation marks omitted).

Like the Hahns, the Greens believe that life begins at conception and that it would violate their religion to facilitate access to contraceptive drugs or devices that operate after that point. 723 F. 3d, at 1122. They specifically object to the same four contraceptive methods as the Hahns and, like the Hahns, they have no objection to the other 16 FDA-approved methods of birth control. *Id.*, at 1125. Although their group-health-insurance plan predates the enactment of ACA, it is not a grandfathered plan because Hobby Lobby elected not to retain grandfathered status before the contraceptive mandate was proposed. *Id.*, at 1124.

The Greens, Hobby Lobby, and Mardel sued HHS and other federal agencies and officials to challenge the contraceptive mandate under RFRA and the Free Exercise Clause.[16] The District Court denied a preliminary injunction, see 870 F. Supp. 2d 1278 (WD Okla. 2012), and the plaintiffs appealed, moving for initial en banc consideration. The Tenth Circuit granted that motion and reversed in a divided opinion. Contrary to the conclusion of the Third Circuit, the Tenth Circuit held that the Greens' two for-profit businesses are "persons" within the meaning of RFRA and therefore may bring suit under that law.

The court then held that the corporations had established a likelihood of success on their RFRA claim. 723 F. 3d, at 1140–1147. The court concluded that the contraceptive mandate substantially burdened the exercise of religion by requiring the companies to choose between "compromis[ing] their religious beliefs" and paying a heavy fee—either "close to $475 million more in taxes every year" if they simply refused to provide coverage for the contraceptives at issue, or "roughly $26 million" annually if they "drop[ped] health-insurance benefits for all employees." *Id.*, at 1141.

The court next held that HHS had failed to demonstrate a compelling interest in enforcing the mandate against the Greens' businesses and, in the alternative, that HHS had failed to prove that enforcement of the mandate was the "least restrictive means" of furthering the Government's asserted interests. *Id.*, at 1143–1144 (emphasis deleted; internal quotation marks omitted). After concluding that the companies had "demonstrated irreparable harm," the court reversed and remanded for the District Court to consider the remaining factors of the preliminaryinjunction test. *Id.*, at 1147.[17]

We granted certiorari. 571 U. S. _____ (2013).

III

A

RFRA prohibits the "Government [from] substantially burden[ing] *a person's* exercise of religion even if the burden results from a rule of general applicability" unless the Government "demonstrates that application of the burden to *the person*—(1) is in furtherance of a compelling governmental interest; and (2) is the least restrictive means of furthering that compelling governmental interest." 42 U. S. C. §§2000bb–1(a), (b) (emphasis added). The first question that we must address is whether this provision applies to regulations that govern the activities of for-profit corporations like Hobby Lobby, Conestoga, and Mardel.

HHS contends that neither these companies nor their owners can even be heard under RFRA. According to HHS, the companies cannot sue because they seek to make a profit for their owners, and the owners cannot be heard because the regulations, at least as a formal matter, apply only to the companies and not to the owners as individuals. HHS's argument would have dramatic consequences.

Consider this Court's decision in *Braunfeld* v. *Brown*, 366 U. S. 599 (1961) (plurality opinion). In that case, five Orthodox Jewish merchants who ran small retail businesses in Philadelphia challenged a Pennsylvania Sunday closing law as a violation of the Free Exercise Clause. Because of their faith, these merchants closed their shops on Saturday, and they argued that requiring them to remain shut on Sunday threatened them with financial ruin. The Court entertained their claim (although it ruled against them on the merits), and if a similar claim were raised today under RFRA against a jurisdiction still subject to the Act (for example, the District of Columbia, see 42 U. S. C. §2000bb–2(2)), the merchants would be entitled to be heard. According to HHS, however, if these merchants chose to incorporate their businesses—without in any way changing the size or nature of their businesses—they would forfeit all RFRA (and free-exercise) rights. HHS would put these merchants to a difficult choice: either give up the right to seek judicial protection of their religious liberty or forgo the benefits, available to their competitors, of operating as corporations.

As we have seen, RFRA was designed to provide very broad protection for religious liberty. By enacting RFRA, Congress went far beyond what this Court has held is constitutionally required.[18] Is there any reason to think that the Congress that enacted such sweeping protection put small-business owners to the choice that HHS suggests? An examination of RFRA's text, to which we turn in the next part of this opinion, reveals that Congress did no such thing.

As we will show, Congress provided protection for people like the Hahns and Greens by employing a familiar legal fiction: It included corporations within RFRA's definition of "persons." But it is important to keep in mind that the purpose of this fiction is to provide protection for human beings. A corporation is simply a form of organization used by human beings to achieve desired ends. An established body of law specifies the rights and obligations of the *people* (including shareholders, officers, and employees) who are associated with a corporation in one way or another. When rights, whether constitutional or statutory, are extended to corporations, the purpose is to protect the rights of these people. For example, extending Fourth Amendment protection to corporations protects the privacy interests of employees and others associated with the company. Protecting corporations from government seizure of their property without just compensation protects all those who have a stake in the corporations' financial well-being. And protecting the free-exercise rights of corporations like Hobby Lobby, Conestoga, and Mardel protects the religious liberty of the humans who own and control those companies.

In holding that Conestoga, as a "secular, for-profit corporation," lacks RFRA protection, the Third Circuit wrote as follows:

> "General business corporations do not, *separate and apart from the actions or belief systems of their indi vidual owners or employees,* exercise religion. They do not pray, worship, observe sacraments or take other religiously-motivated actions separate and apart from the intention and direction of their individual actors." 724 F. 3d, at 385 (emphasis added).

All of this is true—but quite beside the point. Corporations, "separate and apart from" the human beings who own, run, and are employed by them, cannot do anything at all.

B

1

As we noted above, RFRA applies to "a person's" exercise of religion, 42 U. S. C. §§2000bb–1(a), (b), and RFRA itself does not define the term "person." We therefore look to the Dictionary Act, which we must consult "[i]n determining the meaning of any Act of Congress, unless the context indicates otherwise." 1 U. S. C. §1.

Under the Dictionary Act, "the wor[d] 'person' . . . include[s] corporations, companies, associations, firms, partnerships, societies, and joint stock companies, as well as individuals."*Ibid.*; see *FCC* v. *AT&T Inc.*, 562 U. S., (2011) (slip op., at 6) ("We have no doubt that 'person,' in a legal setting, often refers to artificial entities. The Dictionary Act makes that clear"). Thus, unless there is something about the RFRA context that "indicates otherwise," the Dictionary Act provides a quick, clear, and affirmative answer to the question whether the companies involved in these cases may be heard.

We see nothing in RFRA that suggests a congressional intent to depart from the Dictionary Act definition, and HHS makes little effort to argue otherwise. We have entertained RFRA and free-exercise claims brought by nonprofit corporations, see *Gonzales* v. *O Centro Espírita Beneficiente União do Vegetal*, 546 U. S. 418 (2006) (RFRA); *Hosanna-Tabor Evangelical Lutheran Church and School* v. *EEOC*, 565 U. S. (2012) (Free Exercise); *Church of the Lukumi Babalu Aye, Inc.* v. *Hialeah*, 508 U. S. 520 (1993) (Free Exercise), and HHS concedes that a nonprofit corporation can be a "person" within the meaning of RFRA. See Brief for HHS in No. 13–354, at 17; Reply Brief in No. 13–354, at 7–8.[19]

This concession effectively dispatches any argument that the term "person" as used in RFRA does not reach the closely held corporations involved in these cases. No known understanding of the term "person" includes *some* but not all corporations. The term "person" sometimes encompasses artificial persons (as the Dictionary Act instructs), and it sometimes is limited to natural persons. But no conceivable definition of the term includes natural persons and nonprofit corporations, but not for-profit corporations.[20] Cf. *Clark* v. *Martinez*, 543 U. S. 371, 378 (2005) ("To give th[e] same words a different meaning for each category would be to invent a statute rather than interpret one").

2

The principal argument advanced by HHS and the principal dissent regarding RFRA protection for Hobby Lobby, Conestoga, and Mardel focuses not on the statutory term "person," but on the phrase "exercise of religion." According to HHS and the dissent, these corporations are not protected by RFRA because they cannot exercise religion. Neither HHS nor the dissent, however, provides any persuasive explanation for this conclusion.

Is it because of the corporate form? The corporate form alone cannot provide the explanation because, as we have pointed out, HHS concedes that nonprofit corporations can be protected by RFRA. The dissent suggests that nonprofit corporations are special because furthering their religious "autonomy . . . often furthers individual religious freedom as well." *Post*, at 15 (quoting *Corporation of Presiding Bishop of Church of Jesus Christ of Latter-day Saints* v. *Amos*, 483 U. S. 327, 342 (1987) (Brennan, J., concurring in judgment)). But this principle applies equally to for-profit corporations: Furthering their religious freedom also "furthers individual religious freedom." In these cases, for example, allowing Hobby Lobby, Conestoga, and Mardel to assert RFRA claims protects the religious liberty of the Greens and the Hahns.[21]

If the corporate form is not enough, what about the profit-making objective? In *Braunfeld*, 366 U. S. 599, we entertained the free-exercise claims of individuals who were attempting to make a profit as retail merchants, and the Court never even hinted that this objective precluded their claims. As the Court explained in a later case, the "exercise of religion" involves "not only belief and profession but the performance of (or abstention from) physical acts" that are "engaged in for religious reasons." *Smith*, 494 U. S., at 877. Business practices that are compelled or limited by the tenets of a religious doctrine fall comfortably within that definition. Thus, a law that "operates so as to make the practice of . . . religious beliefs more expensive" in the context of business activities imposes a burden on the exercise of religion. *Braunfeld*, *supra*, at 605; see *United States* v. *Lee*, 455 U. S. 252, 257 (1982) (recognizing that "compulsory participation in the social security system interferes with [Amish employers'] free exercise rights").

If, as *Braunfeld* recognized, a sole proprietorship that seeks to make a profit may assert a free-exercise claim,[22] why can't Hobby Lobby, Conestoga, and Mardel do the same?

Some lower court judges have suggested that RFRA does not protect for-profit corporations because the purpose of such corporations is simply to make money.[23] This argument flies in the face of modern corporate law. "Each American jurisdiction today either expressly or by implication authorizes corporations to be formed under its general corporation act for *any lawful purpose* or business." 1 J. Cox & T. Hazen, Treatise of the Law of Corporations §4:1, p. 224 (3d ed. 2010) (emphasis added); see 1A W. Fletcher, Cyclopedia of the Law of Corporations §102 (rev. ed. 2010). While it is certainly true that a central objective of for-profit corporations is to make money, modern corporate law does not require for-profit corporations to pursue profit at the expense of everything else, and many do not do so. For-profit corporations, with ownership approval, support a wide variety of charitable causes, and it is not at all uncommon for such corporations to further humanitarian and other altruistic objectives. Many examples come readily to mind. So long as its owners agree, a for-profit corporation may take costly pollution-control and energy-conservation measures that go beyond what the law requires. A for-profit corporation that operates facilities in other countries may exceed the requirements of local law regarding working conditions and benefits. If for-profit corporations may pursue such worthy objectives, there is no apparent reason why they may not further religious objectives as well.

HHS would draw a sharp line between nonprofit corporations (which, HHS concedes, are protected by RFRA) and for-profit corporations (which HHS would leave unprotected), but the actual picture is less clear-cut. Not all corporations that decline to organize as nonprofits do so in order to maximize profit. For example, organizations with religious and charitable aims might organize as for-profit corporations because of the potential advantages of that corporate form, such as the freedom to participate in lobbying for legislation or campaigning for political candidates who promote their religious or charitable goals.[24] In fact, recognizing the inherent compatibility between establishing a for-profit corporation and pursuing nonprofit goals, States have increasingly adopted laws formally recognizing hybrid corporate forms. Over half of the States, for instance, now recognize the "benefit corporation," a dual-purpose entity that seeks to achieve both a benefit for the public and a profit for its owners.[25]

In any event, the objectives that may properly be pursued by the companies in these cases are governed by the laws of the States in which they were incorporated— Pennsylvania and Oklahoma—and the laws of those States permit for-profit corporations to pursue "any lawful purpose" or "act," including the pursuit of profit in conformity with the owners' religious principles. 15 Pa. Cons. Stat. §1301 (2001) ("Corporations may be incorporated under this subpart for any lawful purpose or purposes"); Okla. Stat., Tit. 18, §§1002, 1005 (West 2012) ("[E]very corporation, whether profit or not for profit" may "be incorporated or organized . . . to conduct or promote any lawful business or purposes"); see also §1006(A)(3); Brief for State of Oklahoma as *Amicus Curiae* in No. 13–354.

3

HHS and the principal dissent make one additional argument in an effort to show that a for-profit corporation cannot engage in the "exercise of religion" within the meaning of RFRA: HHS argues that RFRA did no more than codify this Court's pre-*Smith* Free Exercise Clause precedents, and because none of those cases squarely held that a for-profit corporation has free-exercise rights, RFRA does not confer such protection. This argument has many flaws.

First, nothing in the text of RFRA as originally enacted suggested that the statutory phrase "exercise of religion under the First Amendment" was meant to be tied to this Court's pre-*Smith* interpretation of that Amendment. When first enacted, RFRA defined the "exercise of religion" to mean "the exercise of religion under the First Amendment"—not the exercise of religion as recognized only by then-existing Supreme Court precedents. 42 U. S. C. §2000bb–2(4) (1994 ed.). When Congress wants to link the meaning of a statutory provision to a body of this Court's case law, it knows how to do so. See, *e.g.*, Antiterrorism and Effective Death Penalty Act of 1996, 28 U. S. C. §2254(d)(1) (authorizing habeas relief from a state-court decision that "was contrary to, or involved an unreasonable application of, clearly established Federal law, as determined by the Supreme Court of the United States").

Second, if the original text of RFRA was not clear enough on this point—and we think it was—the amendment of RFRA through RLUIPA surely dispels any doubt. That amendment deleted the prior reference to the First Amendment, see 42 U. S. C. §2000bb–2(4) (2000 ed.) (incorporating §2000cc–5), and neither HHS nor the principal dissent can explain why Congress did this if it wanted to tie RFRA coverage tightly to the specific holdings of our pre-*Smith* free-exercise cases. Moreover, as discussed, the amendment went further, providing that the exercise of religion "shall be construed in favor of a broad protection of religious exercise, to the maximum extent permitted by the terms of this chapter and the Constitution." §2000cc–3(g). It is simply not possible to read these provisions as restricting the concept of the "exercise of religion" to those practices specifically addressed in our pre-*Smith* decisions.

Third, the one pre-*Smith* case involving the free-exercise rights of a for-profit corporation suggests, if anything, that for-profit corporations possess such rights. In *Gallagher* v. *Crown Kosher Super Market of Mass., Inc.*, 366 U. S. 617 (1961), the Massachusetts Sunday closing law was challenged by a kosher market that was organized as a for-profit corporation, by customers of the market, and by a rabbi. The Commonwealth argued that the corporation lacked "standing" to assert a free-exercise claim,[26] but not one member of the Court expressed agreement with that argument. The plurality opinion for four Justices rejected the First Amendment claim on the merits based on the reasoning in *Braunfeld*, and reserved decision on the question whether the corporation had "standing" to raise the claim. See 366 U. S., at 631. The three dissenters, Justices Douglas, Brennan, and Stewart, found the law unconstitutional as applied to the corporation and the other challengers and thus implicitly recognized their right to assert a free-exercise claim. See *id.*, at 642 (Brennan, J., joined by Stewart, J., dissenting); *McGowan* v. *Maryland*, 366 U. S. 420, 578–579 (1961) (Douglas, J., dissenting as to related cases including *Gallagher*). Finally, Justice Frankfurter's opinion, which was joined by Justice Harlan, upheld the Massachusetts law on the merits but did not question or reserve decision on the issue of the right of the corporation or any of the other challengers to be heard. See *McGowan*, 366 U. S., at 521–522. It is quite a stretch to argue that RFRA, a law enacted to provide very broad protection for religious liberty, left for-profit corporations unprotected simply because in *Gallagher*—the only pre-*Smith* case in which the issue was raised—a majority of the Justices did not find it necessary to decide whether the kosher market's corporate status barred it from raising a free-exercise claim.

Finally, the results would be absurd if RFRA merely restored this Court's pre-*Smith* decisions in ossified form and did not allow a plaintiff to raise a RFRA claim unless that plaintiff fell within a category of plaintiffs one of whom had brought a free-exercise claim that this Court entertained in the years before *Smith.* For example, we are not aware of any pre-*Smith* case in which this Court entertained a free-exercise claim brought by a resident noncitizen. Are such persons also beyond RFRA's protective reach simply because the Court never addressed their rights before *Smith*?

Presumably in recognition of the weakness of this argument, both HHS and the principal dissent fall back on the broader contention that the Nation lacks a tradition of exempting for-profit corporations from generally applicable laws. By contrast, HHS contends, statutes like Title VII, 42 U. S. C. §2000e–19(A), expressly exempt churches and other nonprofit religious institutions but not for-profit corporations. See Brief for HHS in No. 13–356, p. 26. In making this argument, however, HHS did not call to our attention the fact that some federal statutes *do* exempt categories of entities that include for-profit corporations from laws that would otherwise require these entities to engage in activities to which they object on grounds of conscience. See, *e.g.*, 42 U. S. C. §300a–7(b)(2); §238n(a).[27] If Title VII and similar laws show anything, it is that Congress speaks with specificity when it intends a religious accommodation not to extend to for-profit corporations.

4

Finally, HHS contends that Congress could not have wanted RFRA to apply to for-profit corporations because it is difficult as a practical matter to ascertain the sincere "beliefs" of a corporation. HHS goes so far as to raise the specter of "divisive, polarizing proxy battles over the religious identity of large, publicly traded corporations such as IBM or General Electric." Brief for HHS in No. 13–356, at 30.

These cases, however, do not involve publicly traded corporations, and it seems unlikely that the sort of corporate giants to which HHS refers will often assert RFRA claims. HHS has not pointed to any example of a publicly traded corporation asserting RFRA rights, and numerous practical restraints would likely prevent that from occurring. For example, the idea that unrelated shareholders— including institutional investors with their own set of stakeholders—would agree to run a corporation under the same religious beliefs seems improbable. In any event, we have no occasion in these cases to consider RFRA's applicability to such companies. The companies in the cases before us are closely held corporations, each owned and controlled by members of a single family, and no one has disputed the sincerity of their religious beliefs.[28]

HHS has also provided no evidence that the purported problem of determining the sincerity of an asserted religious belief moved Congress to exclude for-profit corporations from RFRA's protection. On the contrary, the scope of RLUIPA shows that Congress was confident of the ability of the federal courts to weed out insincere claims. RLUIPA applies to "institutionalized persons," a category that consists primarily of prisoners, and by the time of RLUIPA's enactment, the propensity of some prisoners to assert claims of dubious sincerity was well documented.[29] Nevertheless, after our decision in *City of Boerne*, Congress enacted RLUIPA to preserve the right of prisoners to raise religious liberty claims. If Congress thought that the federal courts were up to the job of dealing with insincere prisoner claims, there is no reason to believe that Congress limited RFRA's reach out of concern for the seemingly less difficult task of doing the same in corporate cases. And if, as HHS seems to concede, Congress wanted RFRA to apply to nonprofit corporations, see, Reply Brief in No. 13–354, at 7–8, what reason is there to think that Congress believed that spotting insincere claims would be tougher in cases involving for-profits?

HHS and the principal dissent express concern about the possibility of disputes among the owners of corporations, but that is not a problem that arises because of RFRA or that is unique to this context. The owners of closely held corporations may—and sometimes do—disagree about the conduct of business. 1 Treatise of the Law of Corporations §14:11. And even if RFRA did not exist, the owners of a company might well have a dispute relating to religion. For example, some might want a company's stores to remain open on the Sabbath in order to make more money, and others might want the stores to close for religious reasons. State corporate law provides a ready means for resolving any conflicts by, for example, dictating how a corporation can establish its governing structure. See, *e.g.*, *ibid; id.*, §3:2; Del. Code Ann., Tit. 8, §351 (2011) (providing that certificate of incorporation may provide how "the business of the corporation shall be managed"). Courts will turn to that structure and the underlying state law in resolving disputes.

For all these reasons, we hold that a federal regulation's restriction on the activities of a for-profit closely held corporation must comply with RFRA.[30]

IV

Because RFRA applies in these cases, we must next ask whether the HHS contraceptive mandate "substantially burden[s]" the exercise of religion. 42 U. S. C. §2000bb–1(a). We have little trouble concluding that it does.

A

As we have noted, the Hahns and Greens have a sincere religious belief that life begins at conception. They therefore object on religious grounds to providing health insurance that covers methods of birth control that, as HHS acknowledges, see Brief for HHS in No. 13–354, at 9, n. 4, may result in the destruction of an embryo. By requiring the Hahns and Greens and their companies to arrange for such coverage, the HHS mandate demands that they engage in conduct that seriously violates their religious beliefs.

If the Hahns and Greens and their companies do not yield to this demand, the economic consequences will be severe. If the companies continue to offer group health plans that do not cover the contraceptives at issue, they will be taxed $100 per day for each affected individual. 26 U. S. C. §4980D. For Hobby Lobby, the bill could amount to $1.3 million per day or about $475 million per year; for Conestoga, the assessment could be $90,000 per day or $33 million per year; and for Mardel, it could be $40,000 per day or about $15 million per year. These sums are surely substantial.

It is true that the plaintiffs could avoid these assessments by dropping insurance coverage altogether and thus forcing their employees to obtain health insurance on one of the exchanges established under ACA. But if at least one of their full-time employees were to qualify for a subsidy on one of the government-run exchanges, this course would also entail substantial economic consequences. The companies could face penalties of $2,000 per employee each year. §4980H. These penalties would amount to roughly $26 million for Hobby Lobby, $1.8 million for Conestoga, and $800,000 for Mardel.

B

Although these totals are high, *amici* supporting HHS have suggested that the $2,000 per-employee penalty is actually less than the average cost of providing health insurance, see Brief for Religious Organizations 22, and therefore, they claim, the companies could readily eliminate any substantial burden by forcing their employees to obtain insurance in the government exchanges. We do not generally entertain arguments that were not raised below and are not advanced in this Court by any party, see *United Parcel Service, Inc.* v. *Mitchell*, 451 U. S. 56, 60, n. 2 (1981); *Bell* v. *Wolfish*, 441 U. S. 520, 532, n. 13 (1979); *Knetsch* v. *United States*, 364 U. S. 361, 370 (1960), and there are strong reasons to adhere to that practice in these cases. HHS, which presumably could have compiled the relevant statistics, has never made this argument— not in its voluminous briefing or at oral argument in this Court nor, to our knowledge, in any of the numerous cases in which the issue now before us has been litigated around the country. As things now stand, we do not even know what the Government's position might be with respect to these *amici's* intensely empirical argument.[31] For this same reason, the plaintiffs have never had an opportunity to respond to this novel claim that— contrary to their longstanding practice and that of most large employers— they would be better off discarding their employer insurance plans altogether.

Even if we were to reach this argument, we would find it unpersuasive. As an initial matter, it entirely ignores the fact that the Hahns and Greens and their companies have religious reasons for providing health-insurance coverage for their employees. Before the advent of ACA, they were not legally compelled to provide insurance, but they nevertheless did so—in part, no doubt, for conventional business reasons, but also in part because their religious beliefs govern their relations with their employees. See App. to Pet. for Cert. in No. 13–356, p. 11g; App. in No. 13–354, at 139.

Putting aside the religious dimension of the decision to provide insurance, moreover, it is far from clear that the net cost to the companies of providing insurance is more than the cost of dropping their insurance plans and paying the ACA penalty. Health insurance is a benefit that employees value. If the companies simply eliminated that benefit and forced employees to purchase their own insurance on the exchanges, without offering additional compensation, it is predictable that the companies would face a competitive disadvantage in retaining and attracting skilled workers. See App. in No. 13–354, at 153.

The companies could attempt to make up for the elimination of a group health plan by increasing wages, but this would be costly. Group health insurance is generally less expensive than comparable individual coverage, so the amount of the salary increase needed to fully compensate for the termination of insurance coverage may well exceed the cost to the companies of providing the insurance. In addition, any salary increase would have to take into account the fact that employees must pay income taxes on wages but not on the value of employer-provided health insurance. 26 U. S. C. §106(a). Likewise, employers can deduct the cost of providing health insurance, see §162(a)(1), but apparently cannot deduct the amount of the penalty that they must pay if insurance is not provided; that difference also must be taken into account. Given these economic incentives, it is far from clear that it would be financially advantageous for an employer to drop coverage and pay the penalty.[32]

In sum, we refuse to sustain the challenged regulations on the ground—never maintained by the Government— that dropping insurance coverage eliminates the substantial burden that the HHS mandate imposes. We doubt that the Congress that enacted RFRA—or, for that matter, ACA—would have believed it a tolerable result to put family-run businesses to the choice of violating their sincerely held religious beliefs or making all of their employees lose their existing healthcare plans.

C

In taking the position that the HHS mandate does not impose a substantial burden on the exercise of religion, HHS's main argument (echoed by the principal dissent) is basically that the connection between what the objecting parties must do (provide health-insurance coverage for four methods of contraception that may operate after the fertilization of an egg) and the end that they find to be morally wrong (destruction of an embryo) is simply too attenuated. Brief for HHS in 13–354, pp. 31–34; *post*, at 22–23. HHS and the dissent note that providing the coverage would not itself result in the destruction of an embryo; that would occur only if an employee chose to take advantage of the coverage and to use one of the four methods at issue.[33] *Ibid.*

This argument dodges the question that RFRA presents (whether the HHS mandate imposes a substantial burden on the ability of the objecting parties to conduct business in accordance with *their religious beliefs*) and instead addresses a very different question that the federal courts have no business addressing (whether the religious belief asserted in a RFRA case is reasonable). The Hahns and Greens believe that providing the coverage demanded by the HHS regulations is connected to the destruction of an embryo in a way that is sufficient to make it immoral for them to provide the coverage. This belief implicates a difficult and important question of religion and moral philosophy, namely, the circumstances under which it is wrong for a person to perform an act that is innocent in itself but that has the effect of enabling or facilitating the commission of an immoral act by another.[34] Arrogating the authority to provide a binding national answer to this religious and philosophical question, HHS and the principal dissent in effect tell the plaintiffs that their beliefs are flawed. For good reason, we have repeatedly refused to take such a step. See, *e.g.*, *Smith*, 494 U. S., at 887 ("Repeatedly and in many different contexts, we have warned that courts must not presume to determine . . . the plausibility of a religious claim"); *Hernandez* v. *Commissioner*, 490 U. S. 680, 699 (1989); *Presbyterian Church in U. S.* v. *Mary Elizabeth Blue Hull Memorial Presbyterian Church*, 393 U. S. 440, 450 (1969).

Moreover, in *Thomas* v. *Review Bd. of Indiana Employment Security Div.*, 450 U. S. 707 (1981), we considered and rejected an argument that is nearly identical to the one now urged by HHS and the dissent. In *Thomas*, a Jehovah's Witness was initially employed making sheet steel for a variety of industrial uses, but he was later transferred to a job making turrets for tanks. *Id.*, at 710. Because he objected on religious grounds to participating in the manufacture of weapons, he lost his job and sought unemployment compensation. Ruling against the employee, the state court had difficulty with the line that the employee drew between work that he found to be consistent with his religious beliefs (helping to manufacture steel that was used in making weapons) and work that he found morally objectionable (helping to make the weapons themselves). This Court, however, held that "it is not for us to say that the line he drew was an unreasonable one." *Id.*, at 715.[35]

Similarly, in these cases, the Hahns and Greens and their companies sincerely believe that providing the insurance coverage demanded by the HHS regulations lies on the forbidden side of the line, and it is not for us to say that their religious beliefs are mistaken or insubstantial. Instead, our "narrow function . . . in this context is to determine" whether the line drawn reflects "an honest conviction," *id.*, at 716, and there is no dispute that it does.

HHS nevertheless compares these cases to decisions in which we rejected the argument that the use of general tax revenue to subsidize the secular activities of religious institutions violated the Free Exercise Clause. See *Tilton* v. *Richardson*, 403 U. S. 672, 689 (1971) (plurality); *Board of Ed. of Central School Dist. No. 1* v. *Allen*, 392 U. S. 236, 248–249 (1968). But in those cases, while the subsidies were clearly contrary to the challengers' views on a secular issue, namely, proper church-state relations, the challengers never articulated a *religious* objection to the subsidies. As we put it in *Tilton*, they were "unable to identify any coercion directed at the practice or exercise of their religious beliefs." 403 U. S., at 689 (plurality opinion); see *Allen*, *supra*, at 249 ("[A]ppellants have not contended that the New York law in any way coerces them as individuals in the practice of their religion"). Here, in contrast, the plaintiffs do assert that funding the specific contraceptive methods at issue violates their religious beliefs, and HHS does not question their sincerity. Because the contraceptive mandate forces them to pay an enormous sum of money—as much as $475 million per year in the case of Hobby Lobby—if they insist on providing insurance coverage in accordance with their religious beliefs, the mandate clearly imposes a substantial burden on those beliefs.

V

Since the HHS contraceptive mandate imposes a substantial burden on the exercise of religion, we must move on and decide whether HHS has shown that the mandate both "(1) is in furtherance of a compelling governmental interest; and (2) is the least restrictive means of furthering that compelling governmental interest." 42 U. S. C. §2000bb–1(b).

A

HHS asserts that the contraceptive mandate serves a variety of important interests, but many of these are couched in very broad terms, such as promoting "public health" and "gender equality." Brief for HHS in No. 13–354, at 46, 49. RFRA, however, contemplates a "more focused" inquiry: It "requires the Government to demonstrate that the compelling interest test is satisfied through application of the challenged law 'to the person'—the particular claimant whose sincere exercise of religion is being substantially burdened." *O'Centro*, 546 U. S., at 430–431 (quoting §2000bb–1(b)). This requires us to "loo[k] beyond broadly formulated interests" and to "scrutiniz[e] the asserted harm of granting specific exemptions to particular religious claimants"—in other words, to look to the marginal interest in enforcing the contraceptive mandate in these cases. *O Centro*, *supra*, at 431.

In addition to asserting these very broadly framed interests, HHS maintains that the mandate serves a compelling interest in ensuring that all women have access to all FDA-approved contraceptives without cost sharing. See Brief for HHS in No. 13–354, at 14–15, 49; see Brief for HHS in No. 13–356, at 10, 48. Under our cases, women (and men) have a constitutional right to obtain contraceptives, see *Griswold* v. *Connecticut*, 381 U. S. 479, 485–486 (1965), and HHS tells us that "[s]tudies have demonstrated that even moderate copayments for preventive services can deter patients from receiving those services." Brief for HHS in No. 13–354, at 50 (internal quotation marks omitted).

The objecting parties contend that HHS has not shown that the mandate serves a compelling government interest, and it is arguable that there are features of ACA that support that view. As we have noted, many employees—those covered by grandfathered plans and those who work for employers with fewer than 50 employees—may have no contraceptive coverage without cost sharing at all.

HHS responds that many legal requirements have exceptions and the existence of exceptions does not in itself indicate that the principal interest served by a law is not compelling. Even a compelling interest may be outweighed in some circumstances by another even weightier consideration. In these cases, however, the interest served by one of the biggest exceptions, the exception for grandfathered plans, is simply the interest of employers in avoiding the inconvenience of amending an existing plan. Grandfathered plans are required "to comply with a subset of the Affordable Care Act's health reform provisions" that provide what HHS has described as "particularly significant protections." 75 Fed. Reg. 34540 (2010). But the contraceptive mandate is expressly excluded from this subset. *Ibid.*

We find it unnecessary to adjudicate this issue. We will assume that the interest in guaranteeing cost-free access to the four challenged contraceptive methods is compelling within the meaning of RFRA, and we will proceed to consider the final prong of the RFRA test, *i.e.*, whether HHS has shown that the contraceptive mandate is "the least restrictive means of furthering that compelling governmental interest." §2000bb–1(b)(2).

B

The least-restrictive-means standard is exceptionally demanding, see *City of Boerne*, 521 U. S., at 532, and it is not satisfied here. HHS has not shown that it lacks other means of achieving its desired goal without imposing a substantial burden on the exercise of religion by the objecting parties in these cases. See §§2000bb–1(a), (b) (requiring the Government to "demonstrat[e] that application of [a substantial] burden to *the person* . . . is the least restrictive means of furthering [a] compelling governmental interest" (emphasis added)).

The most straightforward way of doing this would be for the Government to assume the cost of providing the four contraceptives at issue to any women who are unable to obtain them under their health-insurance policies due to their employers' religious objections. This would certainly be less restrictive of the plaintiffs' religious liberty, and HHS has not shown, see §2000bb–1(b)(2), that this is not a viable alternative. HHS has not provided any estimate of the average cost per employee of providing access to these contraceptives, two of which, according to the FDA, are designed primarily for emergency use. See Birth Control: Medicines to Help You, online at http://www.fda.gov/forconsumers/byaudience/forwomen/freepublications/ucm313215.htm. Nor has HHS provided any statistics regarding the number of employees who might be affected because they work for corporations like Hobby Lobby, Conestoga, and Mardel. Nor has HHS told us that it is unable to provide such statistics. It seems likely, however, that the cost of providing the forms of contraceptives at issue in these cases (if not all FDA-approved contraceptives) would be minor when compared with the overall cost of ACA. According to one of the Congressional Budget Office's most recent forecasts, ACA's insurance-coverage provisions will cost the Federal Government more than $1.3 trillion through the next decade. See CBO, Updated Estimates of the Effects of the Insurance Coverage Provisions of the Affordable Care Act, April 2014, p.2.[36] If, as HHS tells us, providing all women with cost-free access to all FDA-approved methods of contraception is a Government interest of the highest order, it is hard to understand HHS's argument that it cannot be required under RFRA to pay *anything* in order to achieve this important goal.

HHS contends that RFRA does not permit us to take this option into account because "RFRA cannot be used to require creation of entirely new programs." Brief for HHS in 13–354, at 15.[37] But we see nothing in RFRA that supports this argument, and drawing the line between the "creation of an entirely new program" and the modification of an existing program (which RFRA surely allows) would be fraught with problems. We do not doubt that cost may be an important factor in the least-restrictive-means analysis, but both RFRA and its sister statute, RLUIPA, may in some circumstances require the Government to expend additional funds to accommodate citizens' religious beliefs. Cf. §2000cc–3(c) (RLUIPA: "[T]his chapter may require a government to incur expenses in its own operations to avoid imposing a substantial burden on religious exercise."). HHS's view that RFRA can never require the Government to spend even a small amount reflects a judgment about the importance of religious liberty that was not shared by the Congress that enacted that law.

In the end, however, we need not rely on the option of a new, government-funded program in order to conclude that the HHS regulations fail the least-restrictive-means test. HHS itself has demonstrated that it has at its disposal an approach that is less restrictive than requiring employers to fund contraceptive methods that violate their religious beliefs. As we explained above, HHS has already established an accommodation for nonprofit organizations with religious objections. See *supra*, at 9–10, and nn. 8–9. Under that accommodation, the organization can self-certify that it opposes providing coverage for particular contraceptive services. See 45 CFR §§147.131(b)(4), (c)(1); 26 CFR §§54.9815–2713A(a)(4), (b). If the organization makes such a certification, the organization's insurance issuer or third-party administrator must "[e]xpressly exclude contraceptive coverage from the group health insurance coverage provided in connection with the group health plan" and "[p]rovide separate payments for any contraceptive services required to be covered" without imposing "any cost-sharing requirements . . . on the eligible organization, the group health plan, or plan participants or beneficiaries." 45 CFR §147.131(c)(2); 26 CFR §54.9815–2713A(c)(2).[38]

We do not decide today whether an approach of this type complies with RFRA for purposes of all religious claims.[39] At a minimum, however, it does not impinge on the plaintiffs' religious belief that providing insurance coverage for the contraceptives at issue here violates their religion, and it serves HHS's stated interests equally well.[40]

The principal dissent identifies no reason why this accommodation would fail to protect the asserted needs of women as effectively as the contraceptive mandate, and there is none.[41] Under the accommodation, the plaintiffs' female employees would continue to receive contraceptive coverage without cost sharing for all FDA-approved contraceptives, and they would continue to "face minimal logistical and administrative obstacles," *post*, at 28 (internal quotation marks omitted), because their employers' insurers would be responsible for providing information and coverage, see, *e.g.*, 45 CFR §§147.131(c)–(d); cf. 26 CFR §§54.9815–2713A(b), (d). Ironically, it is the dissent's approach that would "[i]mped[e] women's receipt of benefits by 'requiring them to take steps to learn about, and to sign up for, a new government funded and administered health benefit,' " *post*, at 28, because the dissent would effectively compel religious employers to drop health-insurance coverage altogether, leaving their employees to find individual plans on government-run exchanges or elsewhere. This is indeed "scarcely what Congress contemplated." *Ibid.*

C

HHS and the principal dissent argue that a ruling in favor of the objecting parties in these cases will lead to a flood of religious objections regarding a wide variety of medical procedures and drugs, such as vaccinations and blood transfusions, but HHS has made no effort to substantiate this prediction.[42] HHS points to no evidence that insurance plans in existence prior to the enactment of ACA excluded coverage for such items. Nor has HHS provided evidence that any significant number of employers sought exemption, on religious grounds, from any of ACA's coverage requirements other than the contraceptive mandate.

It is HHS's apparent belief that no insurance-coverage mandate would violate RFRA—no matter how significantly it impinges on the religious liberties of employers—that would lead to intolerable consequences. Under HHS's view, RFRA would permit the Government to require all employers to provide coverage for any medical procedure allowed by law in the jurisdiction in question—for instance, third-trimester abortions or assisted suicide. The owners of many closely held corporations could not in good conscience provide such coverage, and thus HHS would effectively exclude these people from full participation in the economic life of the Nation. RFRA was enacted to prevent such an outcome.

In any event, our decision in these cases is concerned solely with the contraceptive mandate. Our decision should not be understood to hold that an insurance-coverage mandate must necessarily fall if it conflicts with an employer's religious beliefs. Other coverage requirements, such as immunizations, may be supported by different interests (for example, the need to combat the spread of infectious diseases) and may involve different arguments about the least restrictive means of providing them.

The principal dissent raises the possibility that discrimination in hiring, for example on the basis of race, might be cloaked as religious practice to escape legal sanction. See *post*, at 32–33. Our decision today provides no such shield. The Government has a compelling interest in providing an equal opportunity to participate in the workforce without regard to race, and prohibitions on racial discrimination are precisely tailored to achieve that critical goal.

HHS also raises for the first time in this Court the argument that applying the contraceptive mandate to for-profit employers with sincere religious objections is essential to the comprehensive health-insurance scheme that ACA establishes. HHS analogizes the contraceptive mandate to the requirement to pay Social Security taxes, which we upheld in *Lee* despite the religious objection of an employer, but these cases are quite different. Our holding in *Lee* turned primarily on the special problems associated with a national system of taxation. We noted that "[t]he obligation to pay the social security tax initially is not fundamentally different from the obligation to pay income taxes." 455 U. S., at 260. Based on that premise, we explained that it was untenable to allow individuals to seek exemptions from taxes based on religious objections to particular Government expenditures: "If, for example, a religious adherent believes war is a sin, and if a certain percentage of the federal budget can be identified as devoted to war-related activities, such individuals would have a similarly valid claim to be exempt from paying that percentage of the income tax." *Ibid.* We observed that "[t]he tax system could not function if denominations were allowed to challenge the tax system because tax payments were spent in a manner that violates their religious belief." *Ibid.*; see *O Centro*, 546 U. S., at 435.

Lee was a free-exercise, not a RFRA, case, but if the issue in *Lee* were analyzed under the RFRA framework, the fundamental point would be that there simply is no less restrictive alternative to the categorical requirement to pay taxes. Because of the enormous variety of government expenditures funded by tax dollars, allowing taxpayers to withhold a portion of their tax obligations on religious grounds would lead to chaos. Recognizing exemptions from the contraceptive mandate is very different. ACA does not create a large national pool of tax revenue for use in purchasing healthcare coverage. Rather, individual employers like the plaintiffs purchase insurance for their own employees. And contrary to the principal dissent's characterization, the employers' contributions do not necessarily funnel into "undifferentiated funds." *Post*, at 23. The accommodation established by HHS requires issuers to have a mechanism by which to "segregate premium revenue collected from the eligible organization from the monies used to provide payments for contraceptive services." 45 CFR §147.131(c)(2)(ii).

Recognizing a religious accommodation under RFRA for particular coverage requirements, therefore, does not threaten the viability of ACA's comprehensive scheme in the way that recognizing religious objections to particular expenditures from general tax revenues would.[43]

In its final pages, the principal dissent reveals that its fundamental objection to the claims of the plaintiffs is an objection to RFRA itself. The dissent worries about forcing the federal courts to apply RFRA to a host of claims made by litigants seeking a religious exemption from generally applicable laws, and the dissent expresses a desire to keep the courts out of this business. See *post*, at 32–35. In making this plea, the dissent reiterates a point made forcefully by the Court in *Smith.* 494 U. S., at 888–889 (applying the *Sherbert* test to all free-exercise claims "would open the prospect of constitutionally required religious exemptions from civic obligations of almost every conceivable kind"). But Congress, in enacting RFRA, took the position that "the compelling interest test as set forth in prior Federal court rulings is a workable test for striking sensible balances between religious liberty and competing prior governmental interests." 42 U. S. C. §2000bb(a)(5). The wisdom of Congress's judgment on this matter is not our concern. Our responsibility is to enforce RFRA as written, and under the standard that RFRA prescribes, the HHS contraceptive mandate is unlawful.

* * *

The contraceptive mandate, as applied to closely held corporations, violates RFRA. Our decision on that statutory question makes it unnecessary to reach the First Amendment claim raised by Conestoga and the Hahns.

The judgment of the Tenth Circuit in No. 13–354 is affirmed; the judgment of the Third Circuit in No. 13–356 is reversed, and that case is remanded for further proceedings consistent with this opinion.

It is so ordered.

KENNEDY, J., Concurring

Nos. 13–354 and 13–356

Sylvia Burwell, Secretary of Health and Human Services, et al., Petitioners

13–354 *v.*

Hobby Lobby Stores, Inc., et al.

On Writ of Certiorari to the United States Court of Appeals for the Tenth Circuit

and

Conestoga Wood Specialties Corporation et al., Petitioners

13–356 *v.*

Sylvia Burwell, Secretary of Health and Human Services, et al.

On Writ of Certiorari to the United States Court of Appeals for the Third Circuit

[June 30, 2014]

JUSTICE KENNEDY, concurring.

It seems to me appropriate, in joining the Court's opinion, to add these few remarks. At the outset it should be said that the Court's opinion does not have the breadth and sweep ascribed to it by the respectful and powerful dissent. The Court and the dissent disagree on the proper interpretation of the Religious Freedom and Restoration Act of 1993 (RFRA), but do agree on the purpose of that statute. 42 U. S. C. §2000bb *et seq.* It is to ensure that interests in religious freedom are protected. *Ante*, at 5–6; *post*, at 8–9 (GINSBURG, J., dissenting).

In our constitutional tradition, freedom means that all persons have the right to believe or strive to believe in a divine creator and a divine law. For those who choose this course, free exercise is essential in preserving their own dignity and in striving for a self-definition shaped by their religious precepts. Free exercise in this sense implicates more than just freedom of belief. See *Cantwell* v. *Connecticut*, 310 U. S. 296, 303 (1940). It means, too, the right to express those beliefs and to establish one's religious (or nonreligious) self-definition in the political, civic, and economic life of our larger community. But in a complex society and an era of pervasive governmental regulation, defining the proper realm for free exercise can be difficult. In these cases the plaintiffs deem it necessary to exercise their religious beliefs within the context of their own closely held, for-profit corporations. They claim protection under RFRA, the federal statute discussed with care and in detail in the Court's opinion.

As the Court notes, under our precedents, RFRA imposes a " 'stringent test.' " *Ante,* at 6 (quoting *City of Boerne* v. *Flores*, 521 U. S. 507, 533 (1997)). The Government must demonstrate that the application of a substantial burden to a person's exercise of religion "(1) is in furtherance of a compelling governmental interest; and (2) is the least restrictive means of furthering that compelling governmental interest." §2000bb–1(b).

As to RFRA's first requirement, the Department of Health and Human Services (HHS) makes the case that the mandate serves the Government's compelling interest in providing insurance coverage that is necessary to protect the health of female employees, coverage that is significantly more costly than for a male employee. *Ante*, at 39; see, *e.g*., Brief for HHS in No. 13–354, pp. 14–15. There are many medical conditions for which pregnancy is contraindicated. See, *e.g., id*., at 47. It is important to confirm that a premise of the Court's opinion is its assumption that the HHS regulation here at issue furthers a legitimate and compelling interest in the health of female employees. *Ante*, at 40.

But the Government has not made the second showing required by RFRA, that the means it uses to regulate is the least restrictive way to further its interest. As the Court's opinion explains, the record in these cases shows that there is an existing, recognized, workable, and already-implemented framework to provide coverage. That framework is one that HHS has itself devised, that the plaintiffs have not criticized with a specific objection that has been considered in detail by the courts in this litigation, and that is less restrictive than the means challenged by the plaintiffs in these cases. *Ante,* at 9–10, and n. 9, 43–44.

The means the Government chose is the imposition of a direct mandate on the employers in these cases. *Ante,* at 8–9. But in other instances the Government has allowed the same contraception coverage in issue here to be provided to employees of nonprofit religious organizations, as an accommodation to the religious objections of those entities. See *ante,* at 9–10, and n. 9, 43–44. The accommodation works by requiring insurance companies to cover, without cost sharing, contraception coverage for female employees who wish it. That accommodation equally furthers the Government's interest but does not impinge on the plaintiffs' religious beliefs. See *ante,* at 44.

On this record and as explained by the Court, the Government has not met its burden of showing that it cannot accommodate the plaintiffs' similar religious objections under this established framework. RFRA is inconsistent with the insistence of an agency such as HHS on distinguishing between different religious believers—burdening one while accommodating the other—when it may treat both equally by offering both of them the same accommodation.

The parties who were the plaintiffs in the District Courts argue that the Government could pay for the methods that are found objectionable. Brief for Respondents in No. 13–354, p. 58. In discussing this alternative, the Court does not address whether the proper response to a legitimate claim for freedom in the health care arena is for the Government to create an additional program. *Ante,* at 41–43. The Court properly does not resolve whether one freedom should be protected by creating incentives for additional government constraints. In these cases, it is the Court's understanding that an accommodation may be made to the employers without imposition of a whole new program or burden on the Government. As the Court makes clear, this is not a case where it can be established that it is difficult to accommodate the government's interest, and in fact the mechanism for doing so is already in place. *Ante,* at 43–44.

"[T]he American community is today, as it long has been, a rich mosaic of religious faiths." *Town of Greece* v. *Galloway*, 572 U. S., (2014) (KAGAN, J., dissenting) (slip op., at 15). Among the reasons the United States is so open, so tolerant, and so free is that no person may be restricted or demeaned by government in exercising his or her religion. Yet neither may that same exercise unduly restrict other persons, such as employees, in protecting their own interests, interests the law deems compelling. In these cases the means to reconcile those two priorities are at hand in the existing accommodation the Government has designed, identified, and used for circumstances closely parallel to those presented here. RFRA requires the Government to use this less restrictive means. As the Court explains, this existing model, designed precisely for this problem, might well suffice to distinguish the instant cases from many others in which it is more difficult and expensive to accommodate a governmental program to countless religious claims based on an alleged statutory right of free exercise. *Ante,* at 45–46.

For these reasons and others put forth by the Court, I join its opinion.

GINSBURG, J., dissenting

Nos. 13–354 and 13–356

Sylvia Burwell, Secretary of Health and Human Services, et al., Petitioners

13–354 *v.*

Hobby Lobby Stores, Inc., et al.

On Writ of Certiorari to the United States Court of Appeals for the Tenth Circuit

and

Conestoga Wood Specialties Corporation et al., Petitioners

13–356 *v.*

Sylvia Burwell, Secretary Of Health And Human Services, et al.

On Writ Of Certiorari To The United States Court Of Appeals for the Third Circuit

[June 30, 2014]

JUSTICE GINSBURG, with whom JUSTICE SOTOMAYOR joins, and with whom JUSTICE BREYER and JUSTICE KAGAN join as to all but Part III–C–1, dissenting.

In a decision of startling breadth, the Court holds that commercial enterprises, including corporations, along with partnerships and sole proprietorships, can opt out of any law (saving only tax laws) they judge incompatible with their sincerely held religious beliefs. See *ante,* at 16–49. Compelling governmental interests in uniform compliance with the law, and disadvantages that religion-based optouts impose on others, hold no sway, the Court decides, at least when there is a "less restrictive alternative." And such an alternative, the Court suggests, there always will be whenever, in lieu of tolling an enterprise claiming a religion-based exemption, the government, *i.e.,* the general public, can pick up the tab. See *ante*, at 41–43.[44]

The Court does not pretend that the First Amendment's Free Exercise Clause demands religion-based accommodations so extreme, for our decisions leave no doubt on that score. See *infra*, at 6–8. Instead, the Court holds that Congress, in the Religious Freedom Restoration Act of 1993 (RFRA), 42 U. S. C. §2000bb *et seq.*, dictated the extraordinary religion-based exemptions today's decision endorses. In the Court's view, RFRA demands accommodation of a for-profit corporation's religious beliefs no matter the impact that accommodation may have on third parties who do not share the corporation owners' religious faith—in these cases, thousands of women employed by Hobby Lobby and Conestoga or dependents of persons those corporations employ. Persuaded that Congress enacted RFRA to serve a far less radical purpose, and mindful of the havoc the Court's judgment can introduce, I dissent.

I

"The ability of women to participate equally in the economic and social life of the Nation has been facilitated by their ability to control their reproductive lives." *Planned Parenthood of Southeastern Pa.* v. *Casey*, 505 U. S. 833, 856 (1992). Congress acted on that understanding when, as part of a nationwide insurance program intended to be comprehensive, it called for coverage of preventive care responsive to women's needs. Carrying out Congress' direction, the Department of Health and Human Services (HHS), in consultation with public health experts, promulgated regulations requiring group health plans to cover all forms of contraception approved by the Food and Drug Administration (FDA). The genesis of this coverage should enlighten the Court's resolution of these cases.

A

The Affordable Care Act (ACA), in its initial form, specified three categories of preventive care that health plans must cover at no added cost to the plan participant or beneficiary.[45] Particular services were to be recommended by the U. S. Preventive Services Task Force, an independent panel of experts. The scheme had a large gap, however; it left out preventive services that "many women's health advocates and medical professionals believe are critically important." 155 Cong. Rec. 28841 (2009) (statement of Sen. Boxer). To correct this oversight, Senator Barbara Mikulski introduced the Women's Health Amendment, which added to the ACA's minimum coverage requirements a new category of preventive services specific to women's health.

Women paid significantly more than men for preventive care, the amendment's proponents noted; in fact, cost barriers operated to block many women from obtaining needed care at all. See, *e.g., id.,* at 29070 (statement of Sen. Feinstein) ("Women of childbearing age spend 68 percent more in out-of-pocket health care costs than men."); *id.,* at 29302 (statement of Sen. Mikulski) ("copayments are [often] so high that [women] avoid getting [preventive and screening services] in the first place"). And increased access to contraceptive services, the sponsors comprehended, would yield important public health gains. See, *e.g., id.,* at 29768 (statement of Sen. Durbin) ("This bill will expand health insurance coverage to the vast majority of [the 17 million women of reproductive age in the United States who are uninsured] . . . . This expanded access will reduce unintended pregnancies.").

As altered by the Women's Health Amendment's passage, the ACA requires new insurance plans to include coverage without cost sharing of "such additional preventive care and screenings . . . as provided for in comprehensive guidelines supported by the Health Resources and Services Administration [(HRSA)]," a unit of HHS. 42 U. S. C. §300gg–13(a)(4). Thus charged, the HRSA developed recommendations in consultation with the Institute of Medicine (IOM). See 77 Fed. Reg. 8725–8726 (2012).[46] The IOM convened a group of independent experts, including "specialists in disease prevention [and] women's health"; those experts prepared a report evaluating the efficacy of a number of preventive services. IOM, Clinical Prevention Services for Women: Closing the Gaps 2 (2011) (hereinafter IOM Report). Consistent with the findings of "[n]umerous health professional associations" and other organizations, the IOM experts determined that preventive coverage should include the "full range" of FDA approved contraceptive methods. *Id.,* at 10. See also *id.,* at 102–110.

In making that recommendation, the IOM's report expressed concerns similar to those voiced by congressional proponents of the Women's Health Amendment. The report noted the disproportionate burden women carried for comprehensive health services and the adverse health consequences of excluding contraception from preventive care available to employees without cost sharing. See, *e.g., id.,* at 19 ("[W]omen are consistently more likely than men to report a wide range of cost-related barriers to receiving . . . medical tests and treatments and to filling prescriptions for themselves and their families."); *id.,* at 103–104, 107 (pregnancy may be contraindicated for women with certain medical conditions, for example, some congenital heart diseases, pulmonary hypertension, and Marfan syndrome, and contraceptives may be used to reduce risk of endometrial cancer, among other serious medical conditions); *id.*, at 103 (women with unintended pregnancies are more likely to experience depression and anxiety, and their children face "increased odds of preterm birth and low birth weight").

In line with the IOM's suggestions, the HRSA adopted guidelines recommending coverage of "[a]ll [FDA-] approved contraceptive methods, sterilization procedures, and patient education and counseling for all women with reproductive capacity."[47] Thereafter, HHS, the Department of Labor, and the Department of Treasury promulgated regulations requiring group health plans to include coverage of the contraceptive services recommended in the HRSA guidelines, subject to certain exceptions, described *infra*, at 25–27.[48] This opinion refers to these regulations as the contraceptive coverage requirement.

B

While the Women's Health Amendment succeeded, a countermove proved unavailing. The Senate voted down the so-called "conscience amendment," which would have enabled any employer or insurance provider to deny coverage based on its asserted "religious beliefs or moral convictions." 158 Cong. Rec. S539 (Feb. 9, 2012); see *id.,* at S1162–S1173 (Mar. 1, 2012) (debate and vote).[49] That amendment, Senator Mikulski observed, would have "pu[t] the personal opinion of employers and insurers over the practice of medicine." *Id.,* at S1127 (Feb. 29, 2012). Rejecting the "conscience amendment," Congress left health care decisions—including the choice among contraceptive methods—in the hands of women, with the aid of their health care providers.

II

Any First Amendment Free Exercise Clause claim Hobby Lobby or Conestoga[50] might assert is foreclosed by this Court's decision in *Employment Div., Dept. of Human Resources of Ore.* v. *Smith*, 494 U. S. 872 (1990). In *Smith*, two members of the Native American Church were dismissed from their jobs and denied unemployment benefits because they ingested peyote at, and as an essential element of, a religious ceremony. Oregon law forbade the consumption of peyote, and this Court, relying on that prohibition, rejected the employees' claim that the denial of unemployment benefits violated their free exercise rights. The First Amendment is not offended, *Smith* held, when "prohibiting the exercise of religion . . . is not the object of [governmental regulation] but merely the incidental effect of a generally applicable and otherwise valid provision." *Id.,* at 878; see *id.,* at 878–879 ("an individual's religious beliefs [do not] excuse him from compliance with an otherwise valid law prohibiting conduct that the State is free to regulate"). The ACA's contraceptive coverage requirement applies generally, it is "otherwise valid," it trains on women's well being, not on the exercise of religion, and any effect it has on such exercise is incidental.

Even if *Smith* did not control, the Free Exercise Clause would not require the exemption Hobby Lobby and Conestoga seek. Accommodations to religious beliefs or observances, the Court has clarified, must not significantly impinge on the interests of third parties.[51]

The exemption sought by Hobby Lobby and Conestoga would override significant interests of the corporations' employees and covered dependents. It would deny legions of women who do not hold their employers' beliefs access to contraceptive coverage that the ACA would otherwise secure. See *Catholic Charities of Sacramento, Inc.* v. *Superior Court*, 32 Cal. 4th 527, 565, 85 P. 3d 67, 93 (2004) ("We are unaware of any decision in which . . . [the U. S. Supreme Court] has exempted a religious objector from the operation of a neutral, generally applicable law despite the recognition that the requested exemption would detrimentally affect the rights of third parties."). In sum, with respect to free exercise claims no less than free speech claims, "'[y]our right to swing your arms ends just where the other man's nose begins.'" Chafee, Freedom of Speech in War Time, 32 Harv. L. Rev. 932, 957 (1919).

III

A

Lacking a tenable claim under the Free Exercise Clause, Hobby Lobby and Conestoga rely on RFRA, a statute instructing that "[g]overnment shall not substantially burden a person's exercise of religion even if the burden results from a rule of general applicability" unless the government shows that application of the burden is "the least restrictive means" to further a "compelling governmental interest." 42 U. S. C. §2000bb–1(a), (b)(2). In RFRA, Congress "adopt[ed] a statutory rule comparable to the constitutional rule rejected in *Smith*." *Gonzales* v. *O Centro Espírita Beneficente União do Vegetal*, 546 U. S. 418, 424 (2006).

RFRA's purpose is specific and written into the statute itself. The Act was crafted to "restore the compelling interest test as set forth in *Sherbert* v. *Verner*, 374 U. S. 398 (1963) and *Wisconsin* v. *Yoder*, 406 U. S. 205 (1972) and to guarantee its application in all cases where free exercise of religion is substantially burdened." §2000bb(b)(1).[52] See also §2000bb(a)(5) ("[T]he compelling interest test as set forth in prior Federal court rulings is a workable test for striking sensible balances between religious liberty and competing prior governmental interests."); *ante,* at 48 (agreeing that the pre-*Smith* compelling interest test is "workable" and "strike[s] sensible balances").

The legislative history is correspondingly emphatic on RFRA's aim. See, *e.g.,* S. Rep. No. 103–111, p. 12 (1993) (hereinafter Senate Report) (RFRA's purpose was "only to overturn the Supreme Court's decision in *Smith,*" not to "unsettle other areas of the law."); 139 Cong. Rec. 26178 (1993) (statement of

Sen. Kennedy) (RFRA was "designed to restore the compelling interest test for deciding free exercise claims."). In line with this restorative purpose, Congress expected courts considering RFRA claims to "look to free exercise cases decided prior to *Smith* for guidance." Senate Report 8. See also H. R. Rep. No. 103–88, pp. 6–7 (1993) (hereinafter House Report) (same). In short, the Act reinstates the law as it was prior to *Smith*, without "creat[ing] . . . new rights for any religious practice or for any potential litigant." 139 Cong. Rec. 26178 (statement of Sen. Kennedy). Given the Act's moderate purpose, it is hardly surprising that RFRA's enactment in 1993 provoked little controversy. See Brief for Senator Murray et al. as *Amici Curiae* 8 (hereinafter Senators Brief) (RFRA was approved by a 97-to-3 vote in the Senate and a voice vote in the House of Representatives).

B

Despite these authoritative indications, the Court sees RFRA as a bold initiative departing from, rather than restoring, pre-*Smith* jurisprudence. See *ante,* at 6, n. 3, 7, 17, 25–27. To support its conception of RFRA as a measure detached from this Court's decisions, one that sets a new course, the Court points first to the Religious Land Use and Institutionalized Persons Act of 2000 (RLUIPA), 42 U. S. C. §2000cc *et seq.,* which altered RFRA's definition of the term "exercise of religion." RFRA, as originally enacted, defined that term to mean "the exercise of religion under the First Amendment to the Constitution." §2000bb–2(4) (1994 ed.). See *ante,* at 6–7. As amended by RLUIPA, RFRA's definition now includes "any exercise of religion, whether or not compelled by, or central to, a system of religious belief." §2000bb–2(4) (2012 ed.) (cross-referencing §2000cc–5). That definitional change, according to the Court, reflects "an obvious effort to effect a complete separation from First Amendment case law." *Ante,* at 7.

The Court's reading is not plausible. RLUIPA's alteration clarifies that courts should not question the centrality of a particular religious exercise. But the amendment in no way suggests that Congress meant to expand the class of entities qualified to mount religious accommodation claims, nor does it relieve courts of the obligation to inquire whether a government action substantially burdens a religious exercise. See *Rasul* v. *Myers*, 563 F. 3d 527, 535 (CADC 2009) (Brown, J., concurring) ("There is no doubt that RLUIPA's drafters, in changing the definition of 'exercise of religion,' wanted to broaden the scope of the kinds of practices protected by RFRA, not increase the universe of individuals protected by RFRA."); H. R. Rep. No. 106–219, p. 30 (1999). See also *Gilardi* v. *United States Dept. of Health and Human Servs.*, 733 F. 3d

1208, 1211 (CADC 2013) (RFRA, as amended, "provides us with no helpful definition of 'exercise of religion.' "); *Henderson* v. *Kennedy*, 265 F. 3d 1072, 1073 (CADC 2001) ("The [RLUIPA] amendments did not alter RFRA's basic prohibition that the '[g]overnment shall not substantially burden a person's exercise of religion.' ").[53]

Next, the Court highlights RFRA's requirement that the government, if its action substantially burdens a person's religious observance, must demonstrate that it chose the least restrictive means for furthering a compelling interest. "[B]y imposing a least-restrictive-means test," the Court suggests, RFRA "went beyond what was required by our pre-*Smith* decisions." *Ante,* at 17, n. 18 (citing *City of Boerne* v. *Flores*, 521 U. S. 507 (1997)). See also *ante,* at 6, n. 3. But as RFRA's statements of purpose and legislative history make clear, Congress intended only to restore, not to scrap or alter, the balancing test as this Court had applied it pre-*Smith*. See *supra,* at 8–9. See also Senate Report 9 (RFRA's "compelling interest test generally should not be construed more stringently or more leniently than it was prior to *Smith*."); House Report 7 (same).

The Congress that passed RFRA correctly read this Court's pre-*Smith* case law as including within the "compelling interest test" a "least restrictive means" requirement. See, *e.g.,* Senate Report 5 ("Where [a substantial] burden is placed upon the free exercise of religion, the Court ruled [in *Sherbert*], the Government must demonstrate that it is the least restrictive means to achieve a compelling governmental interest."). And the view that the pre-*Smith* test included a "least restrictive means" requirement had been aired in testimony before the Senate Judiciary Committee by experts on religious freedom. See, *e.g.,* Hearing on S. 2969 before the Senate Committee on the Judiciary, 102d Cong., 2d Sess., 78–79 (1993) (statement of Prof. Douglas Laycock).

Our decision in *City of Boerne*, it is true, states that the least restrictive means requirement "was not used in the pre-*Smith* jurisprudence RFRA purported to codify." See *ante,* at 6, n. 3, 17, n. 18. As just indicated, however, that statement does not accurately convey the Court's pre*Smith* jurisprudence. See *Sherbert*, 374 U. S., at 407 ("[I]t would plainly be incumbent upon the [government] to demonstrate that no alternative forms of regulation would combat [the problem] without infringing First Amendment rights."); *Thomas* v. *Review Bd. of Indiana Employment Security Div.*, 450 U. S. 707, 718 (1981) ("The state may justify an inroad on religious liberty by showing that it is the least restrictive means of achieving some compelling state interest."). See also Berg, The New Attacks on Religious Freedom Legislation and Why They Are Wrong, 21 Cardozo L. Rev. 415, 424 (1999) ("In *Boerne*, the Court erroneously said that the least restrictive means test 'was not used in the pre-*Smith* jurisprudence.' ").[54]

C

With RFRA's restorative purpose in mind, I turn to the Act's application to the instant lawsuits. That task, in view of the positions taken by the Court, requires consideration of several questions, each potentially dispositive of Hobby Lobby's and Conestoga's claims: Do for-profit corporations rank among "person[s]" who "exercise . . . religion"? Assuming that they do, does the contraceptive coverage requirement "substantially burden" their religious exercise? If so, is the requirement "in furtherance of a compelling government interest"? And last, does the requirement represent the least restrictive means for furthering that interest?

Misguided by its errant premise that RFRA moved beyond the pre-*Smith* case law, the Court falters at each step of its analysis.

1

RFRA's compelling interest test, as noted, see *supra,* at 8, applies to government actions that "substantially burden *a person's exercise of religion.*" 42 U. S. C. §2000bb–1(a) (emphasis added). This reference, the Court submits, incorporates the definition of "person" found in the Dictionary Act, 1 U. S. C. §1, which extends to "corporations, companies, associations, firms, partnerships, societies, and joint stock companies, as well as individuals." See *ante,* at 19–20. The Dictionary Act's definition, however, controls only where "context" does not "indicat[e] otherwise." §1. Here, context does so indicate. RFRA speaks of "a person's *exercise of religion.*" 42 U. S. C. §2000bb–1(a) (emphasis added). See also §§2000bb–2(4), 2000cc–5(7)(a).[55] Whether a corporation qualifies as a "person" capable of exercising religion is an inquiry one cannot answer without reference to the "full body" of pre-*Smith* "free-exercise caselaw." *Gilardi*, 733 F. 3d, at 1212. There is in that case law no support for the notion that free exercise rights pertain to for-profit corporations.

Until this litigation, no decision of this Court recognized a for-profit corporation's qualification for a religious exemption from a generally applicable law, whether under the Free Exercise Clause or RFRA.[56] The absence of such precedent is just what one would expect, for the exercise of religion is characteristic of natural persons, not artificial legal entities. As Chief Justice Marshall observed nearly two centuries ago, a corporation is "an artificial being, invisible, intangible, and existing only in contemplation of law." *Trustees of Dartmouth College* v. *Woodward*, 4 Wheat. 518, 636 (1819). Corporations, Justice Stevens more recently reminded, "have no consciences, no beliefs, no feelings, no thoughts, no desires." *Citizens United* v. *Federal Election Comm'n*, 558 U. S. 310, 466 (2010) (opinion concurring in part and dissenting in part).

The First Amendment's free exercise protections, the Court has indeed recognized, shelter churches and other nonprofit religion-based organizations.[57] "For many individuals, religious activity derives meaning in large measure from participation in a larger religious community," and "furtherance of the autonomy of religious organizations often furthers individual religious freedom as well." *Corporation of Presiding Bishop of Church of Jesus Christ of Latter-day Saints* v. *Amos*, 483 U. S. 327, 342 (1987) (Brennan, J., concurring in judgment). The Court's "special solicitude to the rights of religious organizations," *Hosanna-Tabor Evangelical Lutheran Church and School* v. *EEOC*, 565 U. S., (2012) (slip op., at 14), however, is just that. No such solicitude is traditional for commercial organizations.[58] Indeed, until today, religious exemptions had never been extended to any entity operating in "the commercial, profit-making world." *Amos*, 483 U. S., at 337.[59]

The reason why is hardly obscure. Religious organizations exist to foster the interests of persons subscribing to the same religious faith. Not so of for-profit corporations. Workers who sustain the operations of those corporations commonly are not drawn from one religious community. Indeed, by law, no religion-based criterion can restrict the work force of for-profit corporations. See 42 U. S. C. §§2000e(b), 2000e–1(a), 2000e–2(a); cf. *Trans World Air lines, Inc.* v. *Hardison*, 432 U. S. 63, 80–81 (1977) (Title VII requires reasonable accommodation of an employee's religious exercise, but such accommodation must not come "at the expense of other[employees]"). The distinction between a community made up of believers in the same religion and one embracing persons of diverse beliefs, clear as it is, constantly escapes the Court's attention.[60] One can only wonder why the Court shuts this key difference from sight.

Reading RFRA, as the Court does, to require extension of religion-based exemptions to for-profit corporations surely is not grounded in the pre-*Smith* precedent Congress sought to preserve. Had Congress intended RFRA to initiate a change so huge, a clarion statement to that effect likely would have been made in the legislation. See *Whitman* v. *American Trucking Assns., Inc.*, 531 U. S. 457, 468 (2001) (Congress does not "hide elephants in mouseholes"). The text of RFRA makes no such statement and the legislative history does not so much as mention for-profit corporations. See *Hobby Lobby Stores, Inc.* v. *Sebe lius*, 723 F. 3d 1114, 1169 (CA10 2013) (Briscoe, C. J., concurring in part and dissenting in part) (legislative record lacks "any suggestion that Congress foresaw, let alone intended that, RFRA would cover for-profit corporations"). See also Senators Brief 10–13 (none of the cases cited in House or Senate Judiciary Committee reports accompanying RFRA, or mentioned during floor speeches, recognized the free exercise rights of for-profit corporations).

The Court notes that for-profit corporations may support charitable causes and use their funds for religious ends, and therefore questions the distinction between such corporations and religious nonprofit organizations. See *ante,* at 20–25. See also *ante,* at 3 (KENNEDY, J., concurring) (criticizing the Government for "distinguishing between different religious believers—burdening one while accommodating the other—when it may treat both equally by offering both of them the same accommodation").[61] Again, the Court forgets that religious organizations exist to serve a community of believers. For-profit corporations do not fit that bill. Moreover, history is not on the Court's side. Recognition of the discrete characters of "ecclesiastical and lay" corporations dates back to Blackstone, see 1 W. Blackstone, Commentaries on the Laws of England 458 (1765), and was reiterated by this Court centuries before the enactment of the Internal Revenue Code. See *Terrett* v. *Taylor*, 9 Cranch 43, 49 (1815) (describing religious corporations); *Trustees of Dartmouth College*, 4 Wheat., at 645 (discussing "eleemosynary" corporations, including those "created for the promotion of religion"). To reiterate, "for-profit corporations are different from religious non-profits in that they use labor to make a profit, rather than to perpetuate [the] religious value[s] [shared by a community of believers]." *Gilardi*, 733 F. 3d, at 1242 (Edwards, J., concurring in part and dissenting in part) (emphasis deleted).

Citing *Braunfeld* v. *Brown*, 366 U. S. 599 (1961), the Court questions why, if "a sole proprietorship that seeks to make a profit may assert a free-exercise claim, [Hobby Lobby and Conestoga] can't . . . do the same?" *Ante,* at 22 (footnote omitted). See also *ante,* at 16–17. But even accepting, *arguendo*, the premise that unincorporated business enterprises may gain religious accommodations under the Free Exercise Clause, the Court's conclusion is unsound. In a sole proprietorship, the business and its owner are one and the same. By incorporating a business, however, an individual separates herself from the entity and escapes personal responsibility for the entity's obligations. One might ask why the separation should hold only when it serves the interest of those who control the corporation. In any event, *Braunfeld* is hardly impressive authority for the entitlement Hobby Lobby and Conestoga seek. The free exercise claim asserted there was promptly rejected on the merits.

The Court's determination that RFRA extends to for-profit corporations is bound to have untoward effects. Although the Court attempts to cabin its language to closely held corporations, its logic extends to corporations of any size, public or private.[62] Little doubt that RFRA claims will proliferate, for the Court's expansive notion of corporate personhood—combined with its other errors in construing RFRA—invites for-profit entities to seek religion-based exemptions from regulations they deem offensive to their faith.

2

Even if Hobby Lobby and Conestoga were deemed RFRA "person[s]," to gain an exemption, they must demonstrate that the contraceptive coverage requirement "substantially burden[s] [their] exercise of religion." 42 U. S. C. §2000bb–1(a). Congress no doubt meant the modifier "substantially" to carry weight. In the original draft of RFRA, the word "burden" appeared unmodified. The word "substantially" was inserted pursuant to a clarifying amendment offered by Senators Kennedy and Hatch. See 139 Cong. Rec. 26180. In proposing the amendment, Senator Kennedy stated that RFRA, in accord with the Court's pre-*Smith* case law, "does not require the Government to justify every action that has some effect on religious exercise." *Ibid.*

The Court barely pauses to inquire whether any burden imposed by the contraceptive coverage requirement is substantial. Instead, it rests on the Greens' and Hahns' "belie[f] that providing the coverage demanded by the HHS regulations is connected to the destruction of an embryo in a way that is sufficient to make it immoral for them to provide the coverage." *Ante,* at 36.[63] I agree with the Court that the Green and Hahn families' religious convictions regarding contraception are sincerely held. See *Thomas*, 450 U. S., at 715 (courts are not to question where an individual "dr[aws] the line" in defining which practices run afoul of her religious beliefs). See also 42 U. S. C. §§2000bb–1(a), 2000bb–2(4), 2000cc–5(7)(A).[64] But those beliefs, however deeply held, do not suffice to sustain a RFRA claim. RFRA, properly understood, distinguishes between "factual allegations that [plaintiffs'] beliefs are sincere and of a religious nature," which a court must accept as true, and the "legal conclusion . . . that [plaintiffs'] religious exercise is substantially burdened," an inquiry the court must undertake. *Kaemmerling* v. *Lappin*, 553 F. 3d 669, 679 (CADC 2008).

That distinction is a facet of the pre-*Smith* jurisprudence RFRA incorporates. *Bowen* v. *Roy*, 476 U. S. 693 (1986), is instructive. There, the

Court rejected a free exercise challenge to the Government's use of a Native American child's Social Security number for purposes of administering benefit programs. Without questioning the sincerity of the father's religious belief that "use of [his daughter's Social Security] number may harm [her] spirit," the Court concluded that the Government's internal uses of that number "place[d] [no] restriction on what [the father] may believe or what he may do." *Id.,* at 699. Recognizing that the father's "religious views may not accept" the position that the challenged uses concerned only the Government's internal affairs, the Court explained that "for the adjudication of a constitutional claim, the Constitution, rather than an individual's religion, must supply the frame of reference." *Id.,* at 700–701, n. 6. See also *Hernandez* v. *Commissioner*, 490 U. S. 680, 699 (1989) (distinguishing between, on the one hand, "question[s] [of] the centrality of particular beliefs or practices to a faith, or the validity of particular litigants' interpretations of those creeds," and, on the other, "whether the alleged burden imposed [by the challenged government action] is a substantial one"). Inattentive to this guidance, today's decision elides entirely the distinction between the sincerity of a challenger's religious belief and the substantiality of the burden placed on the challenger.

Undertaking the inquiry that the Court forgoes, I would conclude that the connection between the families' religious objections and the contraceptive coverage requirement is too attenuated to rank as substantial. The requirement carries no command that Hobby Lobby or Conestoga purchase or provide the contraceptives they find objectionable. Instead, it calls on the companies covered by the requirement to direct money into undifferentiated funds that finance a wide variety of benefits under comprehensive health plans. Those plans, in order to comply with the ACA, see *supra,* at 3–6, must offer contraceptive coverage without cost sharing, just as they must cover an array of other preventive services.

Importantly, the decisions whether to claim benefits under the plans are made not by Hobby Lobby or Conestoga, but by the covered employees and dependents, in consultation with their health care providers. Should an employee of Hobby Lobby or Conestoga share the religious beliefs of the Greens and Hahns, she is of course under no compulsion to use the contraceptives in question. But "[n]o individual decision by an employee and her physician—be it to use contraception, treat an infection, or have a hip replaced—is in any meaningful sense [her employer's] decision or action." *Grote* v. *Sebelius*, 708 F. 3d 850, 865 (CA7 2013) (Rovner, J., dissenting). It is doubtful that Congress, when it specified that burdens must be "substantia[l]," had in mind a linkage thus interrupted by independent decisionmakers (the woman and her health counselor) standing between the challenged government action and the religious exercise claimed to be infringed. Any decision to use contraceptives made by a woman covered under Hobby Lobby's or Conestoga's plan will not be propelled by the Government, it will be the woman's autonomous choice, informed by the physician she consults.

3

Even if one were to conclude that Hobby Lobby and Conestoga meet the substantial burden requirement, the Government has shown that the contraceptive coverage for which the ACA provides furthers compelling interests in public health and women's well being. Those interests are concrete, specific, and demonstrated by a wealth of empirical evidence. To recapitulate, the mandated contraception coverage enables women to avoid the health problems unintended pregnancies may visit on them and their children. See IOM Report 102–107. The coverage helps safeguard the health of women for whom pregnancy may be hazardous, even life threatening. See Brief for American College of Obstetricians and Gynecologists et al. as *Amici Curiae* 14–15. And the mandate secures benefits wholly unrelated to pregnancy, preventing certain cancers, menstrual disorders, and pelvic pain. Brief for Ovarian Cancer National Alliance et al. as *Amici Curiae* 4, 6–7, 15–16; 78 Fed. Reg. 39872 (2013); IOM Report 107.

That Hobby Lobby and Conestoga resist coverage for only 4 of the 20 FDA-approved contraceptives does not lessen these compelling interests. Notably, the corporations exclude intrauterine devices (IUDs), devices significantly more effective, and significantly more expensive than other contraceptive methods. See *id.,* at 105.[65] Moreover, the Court's reasoning appears to permit commercial enterprises like Hobby Lobby and Conestoga to exclude from their group health plans all forms of contraceptives. See Tr. of Oral Arg. 38–39 (counsel for Hobby Lobby acknowledged that his "argument . . . would apply just as well if the employer said 'no contraceptives' " (internal quotation marks added)).

Perhaps the gravity of the interests at stake has led the Court to assume, for purposes of its RFRA analysis, that the compelling interest criterion is met in these cases. See *ante,* at 40.[66] It bears note in this regard that the cost of an IUD is nearly equivalent to a month's full-time pay for workers earning the minimum wage, Brief for Guttmacher Institute et al. as *Amici Curiae* 16; that almost one-third of women would change their contraceptive method if costs were not a factor, Frost & Darroch, Factors Associated With Contraceptive Choice and Inconsistent Method Use, United States, 2004, 40 Perspectives on

Sexual & Reproductive Health 94, 98 (2008); and that only one-fourth of women who request an IUD actually have one inserted after finding out how expensive it would be, Gariepy, Simon, Patel, Creinin, & Schwarz, The Impact of Out-ofPocket Expense on IUD Utilization Among Women With Private Insurance, 84 Contraception e39, e40 (2011). See also Eisenberg, *supra,* at S60 (recent study found that women who face out-of-pocket IUD costs in excess of $50 were "11-times less likely to obtain an IUD than women who had to pay less than $50"); Postlethwaite, Trussell, Zoolakis, Shabear, & Petitti, A Comparison of Contraceptive Procurement Preand Post-Benefit Change, 76 Contraception 360, 361–362 (2007) (when one health system eliminated patient cost sharing for IUDs, use of this form of contraception more than doubled).

Stepping back from its assumption that compelling interests support the contraceptive coverage requirement, the Court notes that small employers and grandfathered plans are not subject to the requirement. If there is a compelling interest in contraceptive coverage, the Court suggests, Congress would not have created these exclusions. See *ante,* at 39–40.

Federal statutes often include exemptions for small employers, and such provisions have never been held to undermine the interests served by these statutes. See, *e.g.,* Family and Medical Leave Act of 1993, 29 U. S. C. §2611(4)(A)(i) (applicable to employers with 50 or more employees); Age Discrimination in Employment Act of 1967, 29 U. S. C. §630(b) (originally exempting employers with fewer than 50 employees, 81 Stat. 605, the statute now governs employers with 20 or more employees); Americans With Disabilities Act, 42 U. S. C. §12111(5)(A) (applicable to employers with 15 or more employees); Title VII, 42 U. S. C. §2000e(b) (originally exempting employers with fewer than 25 employees, see *Arbaugh* v. *Y & H Corp.*, 546 U. S. 500, 505, n. 2 (2006), the statute now governs employers with 15 or more employees).

The ACA's grandfathering provision, 42 U. S. C. §18011, allows a phasing-in period for compliance with a number of the Act's requirements (not just the contraceptive coverage or other preventive services provisions). Once specified changes are made, grandfathered status ceases. See 45 CFR §147.140(g). Hobby Lobby's own situation is illustrative. By the time this litigation commenced, Hobby Lobby did not have grandfathered status. Asked why by the District Court, Hobby Lobby's counsel explained that the "grandfathering requirements mean that you can't make a whole menu of changes to your plan that involve things like the amount of co-pays, the amount of coinsurance, deductibles, that sort of thing." App. in No. 13–354, pp. 39–40. Counsel acknowledged that, "just because of economic realities, our plan has to shift over time. I mean, insurance plans, as everyone knows, shif[t] overtime." *Id.,* at 40.[67] The percentage of employees in grandfathered plans is steadily declining, having dropped from 56% in 2011 to 48% in 2012 to 36% in 2013. Kaiser Family Foundation & Health Research & Educ. Trust, Employer Benefits 2013 Annual Survey 7, 196. In short, far from ranking as a categorical exemption, the grandfathering provision is "temporary, intended to be a means for gradually transitioning employers into mandatory coverage." *Gilardi*, 733 F. 3d, at 1241 (Edwards, J., concurring in part and dissenting in part).

The Court ultimately acknowledges a critical point: RFRA's application "*must* take adequate account of the burdens a requested accommodation may impose on non-beneficiaries." *Ante,* at 42, n. 37 (quoting *Cutter* v. *Wil kinson*, 544 U. S. 709, 720 (2005); emphasis added). No tradition, and no prior decision under RFRA, allows a religion-based exemption when the accommodation would be harmful to others—here, the very persons the contraceptive coverage requirement was designed to protect. Cf. *supra,* at 7–8; *Prince* v. *Massachusetts*, 321 U. S. 158, 177 (1944) (Jackson, J., dissenting) ("[The] limitations which of necessity bound religious freedom . . . begin to operate whenever activities begin to affect or collide with liberties of others or of the public.").

4

After assuming the existence of compelling government interests, the Court holds that the contraceptive coverage requirement fails to satisfy RFRA's least restrictive means test. But the Government has shown that there is no less restrictive, equally effective means that would both (1) satisfy the challengers' religious objections to providing insurance coverage for certain contraceptives (which they believe cause abortions); and (2) carry out the objective of the ACA's contraceptive coverage requirement, to ensure that women employees receive, at no cost to them, the preventive care needed to safeguard their health and well being. A "least restrictive means" cannot require employees to relinquish benefits accorded them by federal law in order to ensure that their commercial employers can adhere unreservedly to their religious tenets. See *supra,* at 7–8, 27.[68]

Then let the government pay (rather than the employees who do not share their employer's faith), the Court suggests. "The most straightforward [alternative]," the Court asserts, "would be for the Government to assume the cost of providing . . . contraceptives . . . to any women who are unable to obtain them under their health-insurance policies due to their employers' religious objections." *Ante,* at 41. The ACA, however, requires coverage of preventive services through the existing employer-based system of health insurance "so that [employees] face minimal logistical and administrative obstacles." 78 Fed. Reg. 39888. Impeding women's receipt of benefits "by requiring them to take steps to learn about, and to sign up for, a new [government funded and administered] health benefit" was scarcely what Congress contemplated. *Ibid.* Moreover, Title X of the Public Health Service Act, 42 U. S. C. §300 *et seq.*, "is the nation's only dedicated source of federal funding for safety net family planning services." Brief for National Health Law Program et al. as *Amici Curiae* 23. "Safety net programs like Title X are not designed to absorb the unmet needs of . . . insured individuals." *Id.,* at 24. Note, too, that Congress declined to write into law the preferential treatment Hobby Lobby and Conestoga describe as a less restrictive alternative. See *supra,* at 6.

And where is the stopping point to the "let the government pay" alternative? Suppose an employer's sincerely held religious belief is offended by health coverage of vaccines, or paying the minimum wage, see *Tony and Susan Alamo Foundation* v. *Secretary of Labor*, 471 U. S. 290, 303 (1985), or according women equal pay for substantially similar work, see *Dole* v. *Shenandoah Baptist Church*, 899 F. 2d 1389, 1392 (CA4 1990)? Does it rank as a less restrictive alternative to require the government to provide the money or benefit to which the employer has a religion-based objection?[69] Because the Court cannot easily answer that question, it proposes something else: Extension to commercial enterprises of the accommodation already afforded to nonprofit religion-based organizations. See *ante,* at 3–4, 9–10, 43–45. "At a minimum," according to the Court, such an approach would not "impinge on [Hobby Lobby's and Conestoga's] religious belief." *Ante,* at 44. I have already discussed the "special solicitude" generally accorded nonprofit religion-based organizations that exist to serve a community of believers, solicitude never before accorded to commercial enterprises comprising employees of diverse faiths. See *supra,* at 14–17.

Ultimately, the Court hedges on its proposal to align for-profit enterprises with nonprofit religion-based organizations. "We do not decide today whether [the] approach [the opinion advances] complies with RFRA for purposes of all religious claims." *Ante,* at 44. Counsel for Hobby Lobby was similarly noncommittal. Asked at oral argument whether the Court-proposed alternative was acceptable,[70] counsel responded: "We haven't been offered that accommodation, so we haven't had to decide what kind of objection, if any, we would make to that." Tr. of Oral Arg. 86–87.

Conestoga suggests that, if its employees had to acquire and pay for the contraceptives (to which the corporation objects) on their own, a tax credit would qualify as a less restrictive alternative. See Brief for Petitioners in No. 13–356, p. 64. A tax credit, of course, is one variety of "let the government pay." In addition to departing from the existing employer-based system of health insurance, Conestoga's alternative would require a woman to reach into her own pocket in the first instance, and it would do nothing for the woman too poor to be aided by a tax credit.

In sum, in view of what Congress sought to accomplish, *i.e.,* comprehensive preventive care for women furnished through employer-based health plans, none of the proffered alternatives would satisfactorily serve the compelling interests to which Congress responded.

IV

Among the pathmarking pre-*Smith* decisions RFRA preserved is *United States* v. *Lee*, 455 U. S. 252 (1982). Lee, a sole proprietor engaged in farming and carpentry, was a member of the Old Order Amish. He sincerely believed that withholding Social Security taxes from his employees or paying the employer's share of such taxes would violate the Amish faith. This Court held that, although the obligations imposed by the Social Security system conflicted with Lee's religious beliefs, the burden was not unconstitutional. *Id.,* at 260–261. See also *id.,* at 258 (recognizing the important governmental interest in providing a "nationwide . . . comprehensive insurance system with a variety of benefits available to all participants, with costs shared by employers and employees").[71] The Government urges that *Lee* should control the challenges brought by Hobby Lobby and Conestoga. See Brief for Respondents in No. 13–356, p. 18. In contrast, today's Court dismisses *Lee* as a tax case. See *ante,* at 46–47. Indeed, it was a tax case and the Court in *Lee* homed in on "[t]he difficulty in attempting to accommodate religious beliefs in the area of taxation." 455 U. S., at 259.

But the *Lee* Court made two key points one cannot confine to tax cases. "When followers of a particular sect enter into commercial activity as a matter of choice," the Court observed, "the limits they accept on their own conduct as a matter of conscience and faith are not to be superimposed on statutory schemes which are binding on others in that activity." *Id.,* at 261. The statutory scheme of employer-based comprehensive health coverage involved in these cases is surely binding on others engaged in the same trade or business as the corporate challengers here, Hobby Lobby and Conestoga. Further, the Court recognized in *Lee* that allowing a religion-based exemption to a commercial employer would "operat[e] to impose the employer's religious faith on the employees." *Ibid.*[72] No doubt the Greens and Hahns and all who share their beliefs may decline to acquire for themselves the contraceptives in question. But that choice may not be imposed on employees who hold other beliefs. Working for Hobby Lobby or Conestoga, in other words, should not deprive employees of the preventive care available to workers at the shop next door,[73] at least in the absence of directions from the Legislature or Administration to do so.

Why should decisions of this order be made by Congress or the regulatory authority, and not this Court? Hobby Lobby and Conestoga surely do not stand alone as commercial enterprises seeking exemptions from generally applicable laws on the basis of their religious beliefs. See, *e.g., Newman* v. *Piggie Park Enterprises, Inc.*, 256 F. Supp. 941, 945 (SC 1966) (owner of restaurant chain refused to serve black patrons based on his religious beliefs opposing racial integration), aff 'd in relevant part and rev'd in part on other grounds, 377 F. 2d 433 (CA4 1967), aff 'd and modified on other grounds, 390 U. S. 400 (1968); *In re Minnesota ex rel. McClure,* 370 N. W. 2d 844, 847 (Minn. 1985) (born-again Christians who owned closely held, for-profit health clubs believed that the Bible proscribed hiring or retaining an "individua[l] living with but not married to a person of the opposite sex," "a young, single woman working without her father's consent or a married woman working without her husband's consent," and any person "antagonistic to the Bible," including "fornicators and homosexuals" (internal quotation marks omitted)), appeal dismissed, 478 U. S. 1015 (1986); *Elane Photog raphy, LLC* v. *Willock*, 2013–NMSC–040, ____ N. M. ____, 309 P. 3d 53 (for-profit photography business owned by a husband and wife refused to photograph a lesbian couple's commitment ceremony based on the religious beliefs of the company's owners), cert. denied, 572 U. S. ____ (2014). Would RFRA require exemptions in cases of this ilk? And if not, how does the Court divine which religious beliefs are worthy of accommodation, and which are not? Isn't the Court disarmed from making such a judgment given its recognition that "courts must not presume to determine exemptions in cases of this ilk? And if not, how does the Court divine which religious beliefs are worthy of accommodation, and which are not? Isn't the Court disarmed from making such a judgment givenits recognition that "courts must not presume to determine . . . the plausibility of a religious claim"? *Ante*, at 37.

Would the exemption the Court holds RFRA demands for employers with religiously grounded objections to the use of certain contraceptives extend to employers with religiously grounded objections to blood transfusions (Jehovah's Witnesses); antidepressants (Scientologists); medications derived from pigs, including anesthesia, intravenous fluids, and pills coated with gelatin (certain Muslims, Jews, and Hindus); and vaccinations (Christian Scientists, among others)?[74] According to counsel for Hobby Lobby, "each one of these cases . . . would have to be evaluated on its own . . . apply[ing] the compelling interest-least restrictive alternative test." Tr. of Oral Arg. 6. Not much help there for the lower courts bound by today's decision.

The Court, however, sees nothing to worry about. Today's cases, the Court concludes, are "concerned solely with the contraceptive mandate. Our decision should not be understood to hold that an insurance-coverage mandate must necessarily fall if it conflicts with an employer's religious beliefs. Other coverage requirements, such as immunizations, may be supported by different interests (for example, the need to combat the spread of infectious diseases) and may involve different arguments about the least restrictive means of providing them." *Ante,* at 46. But the Court has assumed, for RFRA purposes, that the interest in women's health and well being is compelling and has come up with no means adequate to serve that interest, the one motivating Congress to adopt the Women's Health Amendment.

There is an overriding interest, I believe, in keeping the courts "out of the business of evaluating the relative merits of differing religious claims," *Lee*, 455 U. S., at 263, n. 2 (Stevens, J., concurring in judgment), or the sincerity with which an asserted religious belief is held. Indeed, approving some religious claims while deeming others unworthy of accommodation could be "perceived as favoring one religion over another," the very "risk the Establishment Clause was designed to preclude." *Ibid.* The Court, I fear, has ventured into a minefield, cf. *Spencer* v. *World Vision, Inc.*, 633 F. 3d 723, 730 (CA9 2010) (O'Scannlain, J., concurring), by its immoderate reading of RFRA. I would confine religious exemptions under that Act to organizations formed "for a religious purpose," "engage[d] primarily in carrying out that religious purpose," and not "engaged . . . substantially in the exchange of goods or services for money beyond nominal amounts." See *id.,* at 748 (Kleinfeld, J., concurring).

* * *

For the reasons stated, I would reverse the judgment of the Court of Appeals for the Tenth Circuit and affirm the judgment of the Court of Appeals for the Third Circuit.

BREYER and KAGAN, JJ., Dissenting

Nos. 13–354 and 13–356

Sylvia Burwell, Secretary of Health and Human Services, et al., Petitioners

13–354 *v.*

Hobby Lobby Stores, Inc., et al.

On Writ of Certiorari to the United States Court of Appeals for the Tenth Circuit

and

Conestoga Wood Specialties Corporation et al., Petitioners

13–356 *v.*

Sylvia Burwell, Secretary of Health and Human Services, et al.

On Writ of Certiorari to the United States Court of Appeals for the Third Circuit

[June 30, 2014]

JUSTICE BREYER and JUSTICE KAGAN, dissenting.

We agree with JUSTICE GINSBURG that the plaintiffs' challenge to the contraceptive coverage requirement fails on the merits. We need not and do not decide whether either for-profit corporations or their owners may bring claims under the Religious Freedom Restoration Act of 1993. Accordingly, we join all but Part III–C–1 of JUSTICE GINSBURG'S dissenting opinion.

End Notes

[1] See also *post*, at 8 ("The exemption sought by Hobby Lobby and Conestoga . . . would deny [their employees] access to contraceptive coverage that the ACA would otherwise secure")

[2] The Act defines "government" to include any "department" or "agency" of the United States. §2000bb–2(1).

[3] In *City of Boerne* v. *Flores*, 521 U. S., 507 (1997), we wrote that RFRA's "least restrictive means requirement was not used in the pre*Smith* jurisprudence RFRA purported to codify." *Id.*, at 509. On this understanding of our pre-*Smith* cases, RFRA did more than merely restore the balancing test used in the *Sherbert* line of cases; it provided even broader protection for religious liberty than was available under those decisions.

[4] See, *e.g.*, *Hankins* v. *Lyght*, 441 F. 3d 96, 108 (CA2 2006); *Guam* v. *Guerrero*, 290 F. 3d 1210, 1220 (CA9 2002).

[5] The principal dissent appears to contend that this rule of construction should apply only when defining the "exercise of religion" in an RLUIPA case, but not in a RFRA case. See *post*, at 11, n. 10. That argument is plainly wrong. Under this rule of construction, the phrase "exercise of religion," as it appears in RLUIPA, must be interpreted broadly, and RFRA states that the same phrase, as used in RFRA, means "religious exercis[e] as defined in [RLUIPA]." 42 U. S. C. §2000bb–2(4). It necessarily follows that the "exercise of religion" under RFRA must be given the same broad meaning that applies under RLUIPA.

[6] We will use "Brief for HHS" to refer to the Brief for Petitioners in No. 13–354 and the Brief for Respondents in No. 13–356. The federal parties are the Departments of HHS, Treasury, and Labor, and the Secretaries of those Departments.

[7] Online at http://www.fda.gov/forconsumers/byaudience/forwomen/free-publications/cm313215. htm. The owners of the companies involved in these cases and others who believe that life begins at conception regard these four methods as causing abortions, but federal regulations, which define pregnancy as beginning at implantation, see, *e.g.*, 62 Fed. Reg. 8611 (1997); 45 CFR §46.202(f) (2013), do not so classify them.

[8] In the case of self-insured religious organizations entitled to the accommodation, the third-party administrator of the organization must "provide or arrange payments for contraceptive services" for the organization's employees without imposing any cost-sharing requirements on the eligible organization, its insurance plan, or its employee beneficiaries. 78 Fed. Reg. 39893 (to be codified in 26 CFR §54.9815–2713A(b)(2)). The regulations establish a mechanism for these third-party administrators to be compensated for their expenses by obtaining a reduction in the fee paid by insurers to participate in the federally facilitated exchanges. See 78 Fed. Reg. 39893 (to be codified in 26 CFR §54.9815–2713A (b)(3)). HHS believes that these fee reductions will not materially affect funding of the exchanges because "payments for contraceptive services will represent only a small portion of total [exchange] user fees." 78 Fed. Reg. 39882.

[9] In a separate challenge to this framework for religious nonprofit organizations, the Court recently ordered that, pending appeal, the eligible organizations be permitted to opt out of the contraceptive mandate by providing written notification of their objections to the Secretary of HHS, rather than to their insurance issuers or third-party administrators. See *Little Sisters of the Poor* v. *Sebelius*, 571 U. S. (2014).

[10] While the Government predicts that this number will decline over time, the total number of Americans working for employers to whom the contraceptive mandate does not apply is still substantial, and there is no legal requirement that grandfathered plans ever be phased out.

[11] Online at http://www.whitehouse.gov/files/documents/health_reform_for_small_businesses.pdf.

[12] Mennonite Church USA, Statement on Abortion, online at http://www.mennoniteusa.org/resource-center/resources /statements -and-resolutions/statement-on-abortion/.

[13] The Hahns and Conestoga also claimed that the contraceptive mandate violates the Fifth Amendment and the Administrative Procedure Act, 5 U. S. C. §553, but those claims are not before us.

[14] See, *e.g.*, WebMD Health News, New Morning-After Pill Ella Wins FDA Approval, online at http://www.webmd.com/sex/birth-control/news/20100813/new-morning-after-pill-ella-wins-fda-approval.

[15] The Greens operate Hobby Lobby and Mardel through a management trust, of which each member of the family serves as trustee. 723 F. 3d 1114, 1122 (CA10 2013). The family provided that the trust would also be governed according to their religious principles. *Ibid.*

[16] They also raised a claim under the Administrative Procedure Act, 5 U. S. C. §553.

[17] Given its RFRA ruling, the court declined to address the plaintiffs' free-exercise claim or the question whether the Greens could bring RFRA claims as individual owners of Hobby Lobby and Mardel. Four judges, however, concluded that the Greens could do so, see 723 F. 3d, at 1156 (Gorsuch, J., concurring); *id.*, at 1184 (Matheson, J., concurring in part and dissenting in part), and three of those judges would have granted plaintiffs a preliminary injunction, see *id.*, at 1156 (Gorsuch, J., concurring).

[18] As discussed, n. 3, *supra*, in *City of Boerne* we stated that RFRA, by imposing a least-restrictive-means test, went beyond what was required by our pre-*Smith* decisions. Although the author of the principal dissent joined the Court's opinion in *City of Boerne*, she now claims that the statement was incorrect. *Post*, at 12. For present purposes, it is unnecessary to adjudicate this dispute. Even if RFRA simply restored the status quo ante, there is no reason to believe, as HHS and the dissent seem to suggest, that the law was meant to be limited to situations that fall squarely within the holdings of pre-*Smith* cases. See *infra*, at 25–28.

[19] Cf. Brief for Federal Petitioners in *O Centro*, O. T. 2004, No. 04–1084, p. II (stating that the organizational respondent was "a New Mexico Corporation"); Brief for Federal Respondent in *Hosanna-Tabor*, O. T. 2011, No. 10–553, p. 3 (stating that the petitioner was an "ecclesiastical corporation").

[20] Not only does the Government concede that the term "persons" in RFRA includes nonprofit corporations, it goes further and appears to concede that the term might also encompass other artificial entities, namely, general partnerships and unincorporated associations. See Brief for HHS in No. 13–354, at 28, 40.

[21] Although the principal dissent seems to think that Justice Brennan's statement in *Amos* provides a ground for holding that for-profit corporations may not assert free-exercise claims, that was not Justice Brennan's view. See *Gallagher* v. *Crown Kosher Super Market of Mass., Inc.*, 366 U. S. 617, 642 (1961) (dissenting opinion); *infra*, at 26–27.

[22] It is revealing that the principal dissent cannot even bring itself to acknowledge that *Braunfeld* was correct in entertaining the merchants' claims. See *post,* at 19 (dismissing the relevance of *Braunfeld* in part because "[t]he free exercise claim asserted there was promptly rejected on the merits").

[23] See, *e.g.*, 724 F. 3d, at 385 ("We do not see how a for-profit, 'artificial being,' . . . that was created to make money" could exercise religion); *Grote* v. *Sebelius*, 708 F. 3d 850, 857 (CA7 2013) (Rovner, J. dissenting) ("So far as it appears, the mission of Grote Industries, like that of any other for-profit, secular business, is to make money in the commercial sphere"); *Autocam Corp.* v. *Sebelius*, 730 F. 3d 618, 626 (CA7 2013) ("Congress did not intend to include corporations primarily organized for secular, profit-seeking purposes as 'persons' under RFRA"); see also 723 F. 3d, at 1171–1172 (Briscoe, C. J., dissenting) ("[T]he specific purpose for which [a corporation] is created matters greatly to how it will be categorized and treated under the law" and "it is undisputed that Hobby Lobby and Mardel are for-profit corporations focused on selling merchandise to consumers").

The principal dissent makes a similar point, stating that "[f]or-profit corporations are different from religious nonprofits in that they use labor to make a profit, rather than to perpetuate the religious values shared by a community of believers." *Post*, at 18–19 (internal quotation marks omitted). The first half of this statement is a tautology; for-profit corporations do indeed differ from nonprofits insofar as they seek to make a profit for their owners, but the second part is factually untrue. As the activities of the for-profit corporations involved in these cases show, some for-profit corporations do seek "to perpetuate the religious values shared," in these cases, by their owners. Conestoga's Vision and Values Statement declares that the company is dedicated to operating "in [a] manner that reflects our Christian heritage and the highest ethical and moral principles of business." App. in No. 13–356, p. 94. Similarly, Hobby Lobby's statement of purpose proclaims that the company "is committed to . . . Honoring the Lord in all we do by operating . . . in a manner consistent with Biblical principles." App. in No. 13–354, p. 135. The dissent also believes that history is not on our side because even Blackstone recognized the distinction between "ecclesiastical and lay" corporations. *Post*, at 18. What Blackstone illustrates, however, is that dating back to 1765, there was no sharp divide among corporations in their capacity to exercise religion; Blackstone recognized that even what he termed "lay" corporations might serve "the promotion of piety." 1 W. Blackstone, Commentaries on the Law of England 458–459 (1765). And whatever may have been the case at the time of Blackstone, modern corporate law (and the law of the States in which these three companies are incorporated) allows for-profit corporations to "perpetuat[e] religious values."

[24] See, *e.g.*, M. Sanders, Joint Ventures Involving Tax-Exempt Organizations 555 (4th ed. 2013) (describing Google.org, which "advance[s] its charitable goals" while operating as a for-profit corporation to be able to "invest in for-profit endeavors, lobby for policies that support its philanthropic goals, and tap Google's innovative technology and workforce" (internal quotation marks and alterations omitted)); cf. 26 CFR §1.501(c)(3)–1(c)(3).

[25] See Benefit Corp Information Center, online at http:// www.benefitcorp.net/state-by-state-legislative-status; *e.g.*, Va. Code Ann. §§13.1–787, 13.1–626, 13.1–782 (Lexis 2011) ("A benefit corporation shall have as one of its purposes the purpose of creating a general public benefit," and "may identify one or more specific public benefits that it is the purpose of the benefit corporation to create. . . . This purpose is in addition to [the purpose of engaging in any lawful business]." " 'Specific public benefit' means a benefit that serves one or more public welfare, religious, charitable, scientific, literary, or educational purposes, or other purpose or benefit beyond the strict interest of the shareholders of the benefit corporation . . . ."); S. C. Code Ann. §§33–38–300 (2012 Cum. Supp.), 33–3–101 (2006), 33–38–130 (2012 Cum. Supp.) (similar).

[26] See Brief for Appellants in *Gallagher*, O. T. 1960 No. 11, pp. 16, 28–31 (arguing that corporation "has no 'religious belief' or 'religious liberty,' and had no standing in court to assert that its free exercise of religion was impaired").

[27] The principal dissent points out that "the exemption codified in §238n(a) was not enacted until three years after RFRA's passage." *Post*, at 16, n. 15. The dissent takes this to mean that RFRA did not, in fact, "ope[n] all statutory schemes to religion-based challenges by for-profit corporations" because if it had "there would be no need for a statute-specific, post-RFRA exemption of this sort." *Ibid.*

This argument fails to recognize that the protection provided by §238n(a) differs significantly from the protection provided by RFRA. Section 238n(a) flatly prohibits discrimination against a covered healthcare facility for refusing to engage in certain activities related to abortion. If a covered healthcare facility challenged such discrimination under RFRA, by contrast, the discrimination would be unlawful only if a court concluded, among other things, that there was a less restrictive means of achieving any compelling government interest.

In addition, the dissent's argument proves too much. Section 238n(a) applies evenly to "any health care entity"—whether it is a religious nonprofit entity or a for-profit entity. There is no dispute that RFRA protects religious nonprofit corporations, so if §238n(a) were redundant as applied to for-profit corporations, it would be equally redundant as applied to nonprofits.

[28] To qualify for RFRA's protection, an asserted belief must be "sincere"; a corporation's pretextual assertion of a religious belief in order to obtain an exemption for financial

reasons would fail. Cf., *e.g.*, *United States* v. *Quaintance*, 608 F. 3d 717, 718–719 (CA10 2010).

[29] See, *e.g.*, *Ochs* v. *Thalacker*, 90 F. 3d 293, 296 (CA8 1996); *Green* v. *White*, 525 F. Supp. 81, 83–84 (ED Mo. 1981); *Abate* v. *Walton*, 1996 WL 5320, *5 (CA9, Jan. 5, 1996); *Winters* v. *State*, 549 N. W. 2d 819–820 (Iowa 1996).

[30] The principal dissent attaches significance to the fact that the "Senate voted down [a] so-called 'conscience amendment,' which would have enabled any employer or insurance provider to deny coverage based on its asserted religious beliefs or moral convictions." *Post*, at 6. The dissent would evidently glean from that vote an intent by the Senate to prohibit for-profit corporate employers from refusing to offer contraceptive coverage for religious reasons, regardless of whether the contraceptive mandate could pass muster under RFRA's standards. But that is not the only plausible inference from the failed amendment—or even the most likely. For one thing, the text of the amendment was "written so broadly that it would allow any employer to deny any health service to any American for virtually any reason—*not just for religious objections*." 158 Cong. Rec. S1165 (Mar. 1, 2012) (emphasis added). Moreover, the amendment would have authorized a blanket exemption for religious or moral objectors; it would not have subjected religious-based objections to the judicial scrutiny called for by RFRA, in which a court must consider not only the burden of a requirement on religious adherents, but also the government's interest and how narrowly tailored the requirement is. It is thus perfectly reasonable to believe that the amendment was voted down because it extended more broadly than the pre-existing protections of RFRA. And in any event, even if a rejected amendment to a bill could be relevant in other contexts, it surely cannot be relevant here, because any "Federal statutory law adopted after November 16, 1993 is subject to [RFRA] unless such law *explicitly excludes* such application by reference to [RFRA]." 42 U. S. C. §2000bb–3(b) (emphasis added). It is not plausible to find such an explicit reference in the meager legislative history on which the dissent relies.

[31] Indeed, one of HHS's stated reasons for establishing the religious accommodation was to "encourag[e] eligible organizations to *continue* to offer health coverage." 78 Fed. Reg. 39882 (2013) (emphasis added).

[32] Attempting to compensate for dropped insurance by raising wages would also present administrative difficulties. In order to provide full compensation for employees, the companies would have to calculate the value to employees of the convenience of retaining their employer-provided coverage and thus being spared the task of attempting to find and sign up for a comparable plan on an exchange. And because some but not all of the companies' employees may qualify for subsidies on an exchange, it would be nearly impossible to calculate a salary increase that would accurately restore the status quo ante for all employees.

[33] This argument is not easy to square with the position taken by HHS in providing exemptions from the contraceptive mandate for religious employers, such as churches, that have the very same religious objections as the Hahns and Greens and their companies. The connection between what these religious employers would be required to do if not exempted (provide insurance coverage for particular contraceptives) and the ultimate event that they find morally wrong (destruction of an embryo) is exactly the same. Nevertheless, as discussed, HHS and the Labor and Treasury Departments authorized the exemption from the contraceptive mandate of group health plans of certain religious employers, and later expanded the exemption to include certain nonprofit organizations with religious objections to contraceptive coverage. 78 Fed. Reg. 39871. When this was done, the Government made clear that its objective was to "protec[t]" these religious objectors "from having to contract, arrange, pay, or refer for such coverage." *Ibid.* Those exemptions would be hard to understand if the plaintiffs' objections here were not substantial.

[34] See, *e.g.*, Oderberg, The Ethics of Co-operation in Wrongdoing, in Modern Moral Philosophy 203–228 (A. O'Hear ed. 2004); T. Higgins, Man as Man: The Science and Art of Ethics

353, 355 (1949) ("The general principles governing cooperation" in wrongdoing—*i.e.*, "physical activity (or its omission) by which a person assists in the evil act of another who is the principal agent"—"present troublesome difficulties in application"); 1 H. Davis, Moral and Pastoral Theology 341 (1935) (Cooperation occurs "when A helps B to accomplish an external act by an act that is not sinful, and without approving of what B does").

[35] The principal dissent makes no effort to reconcile its view about the substantial-burden requirement with our decision in *Thomas*.

[36] Online at http://cbo.gov/publication/45231.

[37] In a related argument, HHS appears to maintain that a plaintiff cannot prevail on a RFRA claim that seeks an exemption from a legal obligation requiring the plaintiff to confer benefits on third parties. Nothing in the text of RFRA or its basic purposes supports giving the Government an entirely free hand to impose burdens on religious exercise so long as those burdens confer a benefit on other individuals. It is certainly true that in applying RFRA "courts must take adequate account of the burdens a requested accommodation may impose on nonbeneficiaries." *Cutter* v. *Wilkinson*, 544 U. S. 709, 720 (2005) (applying RLUIPA). That consideration will often inform the analysis of the Government's compelling interest and the availability of a less restrictive means of advancing that interest. But it could not reasonably be maintained that any burden on religious exercise, no matter how onerous and no matter how readily the government interest could be achieved through alternative means, is permissible under RFRA so long as the relevant legal obligation requires the religious adherent to confer a benefit on third parties. Otherwise, for example, the Government could decide that all supermarkets must sell alcohol for the convenience of customers (and thereby exclude Muslims with religious objections from owning supermarkets), or it could decide that all restaurants must remain open on Saturdays to give employees an opportunity to earn tips (and thereby exclude Jews with religious objections from owning restaurants). By framing any Government regulation as benefiting a third party, the Government could turn all regulations into entitlements to which nobody could object on religious grounds, rendering RFRA meaningless. In any event, our decision in these cases need not result in any detrimental effect on any third party. As we explain, see *infra*, at 43–44, the Government can readily arrange for other methods of providing contraceptives, without cost sharing, to employees who are unable to obtain them under their health-insurance plans due to their employers' religious objections.

[38] HHS has concluded that insurers that insure eligible employers opting out of the contraceptive mandate and that are required to pay for contraceptive coverage under the accommodation will not experience an increase in costs because the "costs of providing contraceptive coverage are balanced by cost savings from lower pregnancy-related costs and from improvements in women's health." 78 Fed. Reg. 39877. With respect to self-insured plans, the regulations establish a mechanism for the eligible employers' third-party administrators to obtain a compensating reduction in the fee paid by insurers to participate in the federally facilitated exchanges. HHS believes that this system will not have a material effect on the funding of the exchanges because the "payments for contraceptive services will represent only a small portion of total [federally facilitated exchange] user fees." *Id.*, at 39882; see 26 CFR §54.9815–2713A(b)(3).

[39] See n. 9, *supra*.

[40] The principal dissent faults us for being "noncommital" in refusing to decide a case that is not before us here. *Post*, at 30. The less restrictive approach we describe accommodates the religious beliefs asserted in these cases, and that is the only question we are permitted to address.

[41] In the principal dissent's view, the Government has not had a fair opportunity to address this accommodation, *post*, at 30. n. 27, but the Government itself apparently believes that when it "provides an exception to a general rule for secular reasons (or for only certain religious reasons), [it] must explain why extending a comparable exception to a specific plaintiff for

religious reasons would undermine its compelling interests." Brief for the United States as *Amicus Curiae* in *Holt* v. *Hobbs*, No. 13–6827, p. 10, now pending before the Court.

[42] Cf. 42 U. S. C. §1396s (Federal "program for distribution of pediatric vaccines" for some uninsured and underinsured children).

[43] HHS highlights certain statements in the opinion in *Lee* that it regards as supporting its position in these cases. In particular, HHS notes the statement that "[w]hen followers of a particular sect enter into commercial activity as a matter of choice, the limits they accept on their own conduct as a matter of conscience and faith are not to be superimposed on the statutory schemes which are binding on others in that activity." 455 U. S., at 261. *Lee* was a free exercise, not a RFRA, case, and the statement to which HHS points, if taken at face value, is squarely inconsistent with the plain meaning of RFRA. Under RFRA, when followers of a particular religion choose to enter into commercial activity, the Government does not have a free hand in imposing obligations that substantially burden their exercise of religion. Rather, the Government can impose such a burden only if the strict RFRA test is met.

[44] The Court insists it has held none of these things, for another less restrictive alternative is at hand: extending an existing accommodation, currently limited to religious nonprofit organizations, to encompass commercial enterprises. See *ante,* at 3–4. With that accommodation extended, the Court asserts, "women would still be entitled to all [Food and Drug Administration]-approved contraceptives without cost sharing." *Ante,* at 4. In the end, however, the Court is not so sure. In stark contrast to the Court's initial emphasis on this accommodation, it ultimately declines to decide whether the highlighted accommodation is even lawful. See *ante,* at 44 ("We do not decide today whether an approach of this type complies with RFRA . . . .").

[45] See 42 U. S. C. §300gg–13(a)(1)–(3) (group health plans must provide coverage, without cost sharing, for (1) certain "evidence-based items or services" recommended by the U. S. Preventive Services Task Force; (2) immunizations recommended by an advisory committee of the Centers for Disease Control and Prevention; and (3) "with respect to infants, children, and adolescents, evidence-informed preventive care and screenings provided for in the comprehensive guidelines supported by the Health Resources and Services Administration").

[46] The IOM is an arm of the National Academy of Sciences, an organization Congress established "for the explicit purpose of furnishing advice to the Government." *Public Citizen* v. *Department of Justice*, 491 U. S. 440, 460, n. 11 (1989) (internal quotation marks omitted).

[47] HRSA, HHS, Women's Preventive Services Guidelines, available at http://www.hrsa.gov/womensguidelines/ (all Internet materials as visited June 27, 2014, and available in Clerk of Court's case file), reprinted in App. to Brief for Petitioners in No. 13–354, pp. 43–44a. See also 77 Fed. Reg. 8725–8726 (2012).

[48] 45 CFR §147.130(a)(1)(iv) (2013) (HHS); 29 CFR §2590.715–2713(a)(1)(iv) (2013) (Labor); 26 CFR §54.9815–2713(a)(1)(iv) (2013) (Treasury).

[49] Separating moral convictions from religious beliefs would be of questionable legitimacy. See *Welsh* v. *United States*, 398 U. S. 333, 357–358 (1970) (Harlan, J., concurring in result).

[50] As the Court explains, see *ante,* at 11–16, these cases arise from two separate lawsuits, one filed by Hobby Lobby, its affiliated business (Mardel), and the family that operates these businesses (the Greens); the other filed by Conestoga and the family that owns and controls that business (the Hahns). Unless otherwise specified, this opinion refers to the respective groups of plaintiffs as Hobby Lobby and Conestoga.

[51] See *Wisconsin* v. *Yoder*, 406 U. S. 205, 230 (1972) ("This case, of course, is not one in which any harm to the physical or mental health of the child or to the public safety, peace, order, or welfare has been demonstrated or may be properly inferred."); *Estate of Thornton* v. *Caldor, Inc.*, 472 U. S. 703 (1985) (invalidating state statute requiring employers to accommodate an employee's Sabbath observance where that statute failed to take into account the burden such an accommodation would impose on the employer or other employees). Notably, in construing the Religious Land Use and Institutionalized Persons

Act of 2000 (RLUIPA), 42 U. S. C. §2000cc *et seq.*, the Court has cautioned that "adequate account" must be taken of "the burdens a requested accommodation may impose on nonbeneficiaries." *Cutter* v. *Wilkinson*, 544 U. S. 709, 720 (2005); see *id.*, at 722 ("an accommodation must be measured so that it does not override other significant interests"). A balanced approach is all the more in order when the Free Exercise Clause itself is at stake, not a statute designed to promote accommodation to religious beliefs and practices.

[52] Under *Sherbert* and *Yoder*, the Court "requir[ed] the government to justify any substantial burden on religiously motivated conduct by a compelling state interest and by means narrowly tailored to achieve that interest." *Employment Div., Dept. of Human Resources of Ore.* v. *Smith*, 494 U. S. 872, 894 (1990) (O'Connor, J., concurring in judgment).

[53] RLUIPA, the Court notes, includes a provision directing that "[t]his chapter [*i.e.*, RLUIPA] shall be construed in favor of a broad protection of religious exercise, to the maximum extent permitted by the terms of [the Act] and the Constitution." 42 U. S. C. §2000cc–3(g); see *ante*, at 6–7, 26. RFRA incorporates RLUIPA's definition of "exercise of religion," as RLUIPA does, but contains no omnibus rule of construction governing the statute in its entirety.

[54] The Court points out that I joined the majority opinion in *City of Boerne* and did not then question the statement that "least restrictive means . . . was not used [pre-*Smith*]." *Ante*, at 17, n. 18. Concerning that observation, I remind my colleagues of Justice Jackson's sage comment: "I see no reason why I should be consciously wrong today because I was unconsciously wrong yesterday." *Massachusetts* v. *United States*, 333 U. S. 611, 639–640 (1948) (dissenting opinion).

[55] As earlier explained, see *supra*, at 10–11, RLUIPA's amendment of the definition of "exercise of religion" does not bear the weight the Court places on it. Moreover, it is passing strange to attribute to RLUIPA any purpose to cover entities other than "religious assembl[ies] or institution[s]." 42 U. S. C. §2000cc(a)(1). But cf. *ante*, at 26. That law applies to land-use regulation. §2000cc(a)(1). To permit commercial enterprises to challenge zoning and other land-use regulations under RLUIPA would "dramatically expand the statute's reach" and deeply intrude on local prerogatives, contrary to Congress' intent. Brief for National League of Cities et al. as *Amici Curiae* 26.

[56] The Court regards *Gallagher* v. *Crown Kosher Super Market of Mass., Inc.*, 366 U. S. 617 (1961), as "suggest[ing] . . . that for-profit corporations possess [free-exercise] rights." *Ante*, at 26–27. See also *ante*, at 21, n. 21. The suggestion is barely there. True, one of the five challengers to the Sunday closing law assailed in *Gallagher* was a corporation owned by four Orthodox Jews. The other challengers were human individuals, not artificial, law-created entities, so there was no need to determine whether the corporation could institute the litigation. Accordingly, the plurality stated it could pretermit the question "whether appellees ha[d] standing" because *Braunfeld* v. *Brown*, 366 U. S. 599 (1961), which upheld a similar closing law, was fatal to their claim on the merits. 366 U. S., at 631.

[57] See, *e.g.*, *Hosanna-Tabor Evangelical Lutheran Church and School* v. *EEOC*, 565 U. S. (2012); *Gonzales* v. *O Centro Espírita Benefi cente União do Vegetal*, 546 U. S. 418 (2006); *Church of Lukumi Babalu Aye, Inc.* v. *Hialeah*, 508 U. S. 520 (1993); *Jimmy Swaggart Ministries* v. *Board of Equalization of Cal.*, 493 U. S. 378 (1990).

[58] Typically, Congress has accorded to organizations religious in character religion-based exemptions from statutes of general application. *E.g.*, 42 U. S. C. §2000e–1(a) (Title VII exemption from prohibition against employment discrimination based on religion for "a religious corporation, association, educational institution, or society with respect to the employment of individuals of a particular religion to perform work connected with the carrying on . . . of its activities"); 42 U. S. C. §12113(d)(1) (parallel exemption in Americans With Disabilities Act of 1990). It can scarcely be maintained that RFRA enlarges these exemptions to allow Hobby Lobby and Conestoga to hire only persons who share the religious beliefs of the Greens or Hahns. Nor does the Court suggest otherwise. Cf. *ante*, at 28.

The Court does identify two statutory exemptions it reads to cover for-profit corporations, 42 U. S. C. §§300a–7(b)(2) and 238n(a), and infers from them that "Congress speaks with specificity when it intends a religious accommodation not to extend to for-profit corporations," *ante,* at 28. The Court's inference is unwarranted. The exemptions the Court cites cover certain medical personnel who object to performing or assisting with abortions. Cf. *ante,* at 28, n. 27 ("the protection provided by §238n(a) differs significantly from the protection provided by RFRA"). Notably, the Court does not assert that these exemptions have in fact been afforded to for-profit corporations. See §238n(c) ("health care entity" covered by exemption is a term defined to include "an individual physician, a postgraduate physician training program, and a participant in a program of training in the health professions"); Tozzi, Whither Free Exercise: *Employment Division* v. *Smith* and the Rebirth of State Constitutional Free Exercise Clause Jurisprudence?, 48 J. Catholic Legal Studies 269, 296, n. 133 (2009) ("Catholic physicians, but not necessarily hospitals, . . . may be able to invoke [§238n(a)] . . . ."); cf. S. 137, 113th Cong., 1st Sess. (2013) (as introduced) (Abortion Non-Discrimination Act of 2013, which would amend the definition of "health care entity" in §238n to include "hospital[s]," "health insurance plan[s]," and other health care facilities). These provisions are revealing in a way that detracts from one of the Court's main arguments. They show that Congress is not content to rest on the Dictionary Act when it wishes to ensure that particular entities are among those eligible for a religious accommodation.

Moreover, the exemption codified in §238n(a) was not enacted until three years after RFRA's passage. See Omnibus Consolidated Rescissions and Appropriations Act of 1996, §515, 110 Stat. 1321–245. If, as the Court believes, RFRA opened all statutory schemes to religion-based challenges by for-profit corporations, there would be no need for a statute-specific, post-RFRA exemption of this sort.

[59] That is not to say that a category of plaintiffs, such as resident aliens, may bring RFRA claims only if this Court expressly "addressed their [free-exercise] rights before *Smith*." *Ante,* at 27. Continuing with the Court's example, resident aliens, unlike corporations, are flesh-andblood individuals who plainly count as persons sheltered by the First Amendment, see *United States* v. *Verdugo-Urquidez*, 494 U. S. 259, 271 (1990) (citing *Bridges* v. *Wixon*, 326 U. S. 135, 148 (1945)), and *a fortiori*, RFRA.

[60] I part ways with JUSTICE KENNEDY on the context relevant here. He sees it as the employers' "exercise [of] their religious beliefs within the context of their own closely held, for-profit corporations." *Ante,* at 2 (concurring opinion). See also *ante,* at 45–46 (opinion of the Court) (similarly concentrating on religious faith of employers without reference to the different beliefs and liberty interests of employees). I see as the relevant context the employers' asserted right to exercise religion within a nationwide program designed to protect against health hazards employees who do not subscribe to their employers' religious beliefs.

[61] According to the Court, the Government "concedes" that "nonprofit corporation[s]" are protected by RFRA. *Ante,* at 19. See also *ante,* at 20, 24, 30. That is not an accurate description of the Government's position, which encompasses only "churches," "*religious* institutions," and "*religious* non-profits." Brief for Respondents in No. 13–356, p. 28 (emphasis added). See also Reply Brief in No. 13–354, p. 8 ("RFRA incorporates the longstanding and common-sense distinction between religious organizations, which sometimes have been accorded accommodations under generally applicable laws in recognition of their accepted religious character, and for-profit corporations organized to do business in the commercial world.").

[62] The Court does not even begin to explain how one might go about ascertaining the religious scruples of a corporation where shares are sold to the public. No need to speculate on that, the Court says, for "it seems unlikely" that large corporations "will often assert RFRA claims." *Ante,* at 29. Perhaps so, but as Hobby Lobby's case demonstrates, such claims are indeed pursued by large corporations, employing thousands of persons of different faiths,

whose ownership is not diffuse. "Closely held" is not synonymous with "small." Hobby Lobby is hardly the only enterprise of sizable scale that is family owned or closely held. For example, the family-owned candy giant Mars, Inc., takes in $33 billion in revenues and has some 72,000 employees, and closely held Cargill, Inc., takes in more than $136 billion in revenues and employs some 140,000 persons. See Forbes, America's Largest Private Companies 2013, available at http://www.forbes.com/ largest-private-companies/.

Nor does the Court offer any instruction on how to resolve the disputes that may crop up among corporate owners over religious values and accommodations. The Court is satisfied that "[s]tate corporate law provides a ready means for resolving any conflicts," *ante*, at 30, but the authorities cited in support of that proposition are hardly helpful. See Del. Code Ann., Tit. 8, §351 (2011) (certificates of incorporation may specify how the business is managed); 1 J. Cox & T. Hazen, Treatise on the Law of Corporations §3:2 (3d ed. 2010) (section entitled "Selecting the state of incorporation"); *id.*, §14:11 (observing that "[d]espite the frequency of dissension and deadlock in close corporations, in some states neither legislatures nor courts have provided satisfactory solutions"). And even if a dispute settlement mechanism is in place, how is the arbiter of a religion-based intracorporate controversy to resolve the disagreement, given this Court's instruction that "courts have no business addressing [whether an asserted religious belief] is substantial," *ante*, at 36?

[63] The Court dismisses the argument, advanced by some *amici*, that the $2,000-per-employee tax charged to certain employers that fail to provide health insurance is less than the average cost of offering health insurance, noting that the Government has not provided the statistics that could support such an argument. See *ante*, at 32–34. The Court overlooks, however, that it is not the Government's obligation to prove that an asserted burden is *in*substantial. Instead, it is incumbent upon plaintiffs to demonstrate, in support of a RFRA claim, the substantiality of the alleged burden.

[64] The Court levels a criticism that is as wrongheaded as can be. In no way does the dissent "tell the plaintiffs that their beliefs are flawed." *Ante*, at 37. Right or wrong in this domain is a judgment no Member of this Court, or any civil court, is authorized or equipped to make. What the Court must decide is not "the plausibility of a religious claim," *ante*, at 37 (internal quotation marks omitted), but whether accommodating that claim risks depriving others of rights accorded them by the laws of the United States. See *supra*, at 7–8; *infra*, at 27.

[65] IUDs, which are among the most reliable forms of contraception, generally cost women more than $1,000 when the expenses of the office visit and insertion procedure are taken into account. See Eisenberg, McNicholas, & Peipert, Cost as a Barrier to Long-Acting Reversible Contraceptive (LARC) Use in Adolescents, 52 J. Adolescent Health S59, S60 (2013). See also Winner et al., Effectiveness of Long-Acting Reversible Contraception, 366 New Eng. J. Medicine 1998, 1999 (2012).

[66] Although the Court's opinion makes this assumption grudgingly, see *ante*, at 39–40, one Member of the majority recognizes, without reservation, that "the [contraceptive coverage] mandate serves the Government's compelling interest in providing insurance coverage that is necessary to protect the health of female employees." *Ante*, at 2 (opinion of KENNEDY, J.).

[67] Hobby Lobby's *amicus* National Religious Broadcasters similarly states that, "[g]iven the nature of employers' needs to meet changing economic and staffing circumstances, and to adjust insurance coverage accordingly, the actual benefit of the 'grandfather' exclusion is *de minimis* and transitory at best." Brief for National Religious Broadcasters as *Amicus Curiae* in No. 13–354, p. 28.

[68] As the Court made clear in *Cutter*, the government's license to grant religion-based exemptions from generally applicable laws is constrained by the Establishment Clause. 544 U. S., at 720–722. "[W]e are a cosmopolitan nation made up of people of almost every conceivable religious preference," *Braunfeld*, 366 U. S., at 606, a "rich mosaic of religious faiths," *Town of Greece* v. *Galloway*, 572 U. S., (2014) (KAGAN, J., dissenting) (slip op., at 15).

Consequently, one person's right to free exercise must be kept in harmony with the rights of her fellow citizens, and "some religious practices [must] yield to the common good." *United States* v. *Lee*, 455 U. S. 252, 259 (1982).

[69] Cf. *Ashcroft* v. *American Civil Liberties Union*, 542 U. S. 656, 666 (2004) (in context of First Amendment Speech Clause challenge to a content-based speech restriction, courts must determine "whether the challenged regulation is the least restrictive means among *available*, effective alternatives" (emphasis added)).

[70] On brief, Hobby Lobby and Conestoga barely addressed the extension solution, which would bracket commercial enterprises with nonprofit religion-based organizations for religious accommodations purposes. The hesitation is understandable, for challenges to the adequacy of the accommodation accorded religious nonprofit organizations are currently *sub judice*. See, *e.g., Little Sisters of the Poor Home for the Aged* v. *Sebelius*, F. Supp. 2d, 2013 WL 6839900 (Colo., Dec. 27, 2013), injunction pending appeal granted, 571 U. S. (2014). At another point in today's decision, the Court refuses to consider an argument neither "raised below [nor] advanced in this Court by any party," giving Hobby Lobby and Conestoga "[no] opportunity to respond to [that] novel claim." *Ante,* at 33. Yet the Court is content to decide this case (and this case only) on the ground that HHS could make an accommodation never suggested in the parties' presentations. RFRA cannot sensibly be read to "requir[e] the government to . . . refute each and every conceivable alternative regulation," *United States* v. *Wilgus*, 638 F. 3d 1274, 1289 (CA10 2011), especially where the alternative on which the Court seizes was not pressed by any challenger.

[71] As a sole proprietor, Lee was subject to personal liability for violating the law of general application he opposed. His claim to a religion-based exemption would have been even thinner had he conducted his business as a corporation, thus avoiding personal liability.

[72] Congress amended the Social Security Act in response to *Lee*. The amended statute permits Amish sole proprietors and partnerships (but not Amish-owned corporations) to obtain an exemption from the obligation to pay Social Security taxes only for employees who are coreligionists and who likewise seek an exemption and agree to give up their Social Security benefits. See 26 U. S. C. §3127(a)(2), (b)(1). Thus, employers with sincere religious beliefs have no right to a religion-based exemption that would deprive employees of Social Security benefits without the employee's consent—an exemption analogous to the one Hobby Lobby and Conestoga seek here.

[73] Cf. *Tony and Susan Alamo Foundation* v. *Secretary of Labor*, 471 U. S. 290, 299 (1985) (disallowing religion-based exemption that "would undoubtedly give [the commercial enterprise seeking the exemption] and similar organizations an advantage over their competitors").

[74] Religious objections to immunization programs are not hypothetical. See *Phillips* v. *New York*, _____ F. Supp. 2d _____, 2014 WL 2547584 (EDNY, June 5, 2014) (dismissing free exercise challenges to New York's vaccination practices); Liberty Counsel, Compulsory Vaccinations Threaten Religious Freedom (2007), available at http://www.lc.org/media/9980/attachments/memo_vaccination.pdf.

INDEX

A

B

C

D

E

F

G

H

I

J

L

M

N

O

P

Q

R

S

T

U

V

W

Y